I0161203

THE WRITINGS
OF EMILIE GLEN

1

POEMS
FROM CHAPBOOKS

Selected and edited
by Brett Rutherford

THE POET'S PRESS
Pittsburgh, PA

Copyright 2009 by The Poet's Press
Second Edition, June 2012
Second printing, 2016
www.poetspress.org

ISBN 0-922558-68-X (paperback)
This is the 201st publication of The Poet's Press
Also published in Adobe Acrobat (PDF) format.

Cover art:
Detail of a wood engraving
by John DePol

THE POET'S PRESS
2209 Murray Avenue #3
Pittsburgh, PA 15217

TABLE OF CONTENTS

MAD HATTER (1968)

LATE TO THE KITCHEN (1976)

UP TO US CHICKENS (1972)

HOPE OF AMETHYST (1986)

GLENDA AND HER GUITAR,
EMILIE AND HER PIANO (1991)

RAILS AWAY (1983)

ABOUT THIS BOOK

ABOUT EMILIE GLEN

Meeting Emilie

It was my first Greenwich Village poetry reading. One rainy night in the muggy summer of 1969, I ascended the subway stairs from the Christopher Street station for the first time. Like most very, very young poets I carried a heavy ledger book full of most of my poems, a yellow legal pad, and my hand-bound first chapbook. Using the poetry listings in *The Village Voice*, and the requisite beginner's street map to Manhattan, I walked several blocks east to the Waverly Theater. I was getting close: the right street, almost the right address. Ah, there it was, on a dark metal door: a hand-lettered sign pointing me in and up. In the dimly-lit loft above, I joined a circle of anxious poets, shuffling their papers and waiting their turn to read. They all seemed to know one another, and they were a motley crew, from hippies to aging Beats, from brawny blue-collar types to wispy graybeards.

At the center of the circle, the poet Emilie Glen presided. She was a tall woman, perhaps in her early fifties (so little did I suspect!) with striking red hair, dressed in an odd assortment of clothes, a cross between Baby Jane Hudson and Lolita. Her voice was refined, every syllable crisp and clear, her poems lithe little narratives of New York life, spiced with delicious word play. She read her poetry with us, as one of us, not as one enthroned as judge, critic, gatekeeper.

Emilie — one of the major doyens of the open poetry scene — was adept at making everyone feel welcome. Beginners, mumblers, hopeless versifiers, stray mental patients, and fine poets jostled elbow to elbow at her readings. Everyone had his or her moment in the sun, either in the open "one around" where everyone warmed up by reading just one poem, or, for those who dared, with a full five minutes of self-glorying performance. There was usually a "featured reader" who did two twenty-minute sets, and, naturally, being featured was to attain the pinnacle, your name listed in the newspapers and your work, perhaps, noticed by some visiting publisher, agent or love-of-your-life. And even though the awful and the truly great presented themselves before her, one sensed that she knew the difference. We were all workers in the vineyard, but there was no confusing Ripple with Moët et Chandon. In the New York poetry scene, one quickly learns that bad art is accorded polite silence, while great art is embraced with an ardor that would shock New Englanders.

This was the 1960s-1970s Manhattan poetry scene. Although venues like St. Mark's in the East Village had more celebrity status with their indelible associations with the art scene and underground culture, the West Village had numerous poetry outlets, where a wide mix of styles and degrees of talent blossomed. Ree Dragonette, Emilie's arch-rival, ran a

<15>

poetry-theatre salon from her loft in Westbeth. Other venues includes St. John's in the Village; Poetry on the Piers at Gansevoort Pier on the Hudson; Boruk Glasgow's at his East 14th Street loft, downstairs from a boxing gym (imagine those two groups eyeing one another suspiciously on the stairs!); Risa Korsun's events at a church at St. Mark's Place and at the Baha'i Center; and the New York Poets' Cooperative at various cafes and apartments. Uptown, Marguerite Harris hosted a series at a tavern, Dr. Generosity's, although she frowned upon featuring poets who read "too frequently below 14th Street." Poets and poetry lovers in those days had their choice, on any given night, of a good half-dozen poetry events. Many of these organizations and venues came and went; Emilie Glen's readings and salons, running for more than two decades, outlasted most of them.

The vast majority of these events were listed as "featured and open," which meant that after hearing the featured poet, members of the audience were welcome to share their work. They did, and the most active poets on the scene had the chance to premiere new work, and get practice in front of live audiences, three or four nights a week.

Emilie welcomed me enthusiastically and we soon became friends. For the next two decades, I would see her weekly, sometimes daily. Emilie hosted poets twice a week – Sunday nights at her 77 Columbia Street apartment, and another night at various West Village lofts or theaters. In addition, we would meet at various old-fashioned restaurants: Schrafft's, Macy's Fountain, Rumpelmayers. If I cooked dinner at home, my famous honey-crumb meatloaf was mandatory, after I assured Emilie it contained no "alarming spices." Fortunately she didn't inquire about herbs.

Although she rode to her dinner engagements on a bicycle, dressed in short skirts and pink leotards, red hair flying, Emilie was not the rag-tag Village Bohemian she appeared to be. She had been a child of privilege. Taken on the Grand Tour of Europe as a young girl, she had seen Paris, the Harz Mountains, Rome. Later, her family summered at Chautauqua. She trained as a child prodigy under concert pianist Ernest Hutchison, and continued on to Juilliard School in Manhattan under his tutelage.

Unlike the rest of us, Emilie did not have to go to work on Monday. Or Tuesday. She was provided for, modestly but securely. She was able to do what we all dreamt of: to devote her life to poetry.

Emilie was married, but her husband, Charlie Dash, was absent and seldom mentioned. It was clear from Emilie's carefree ways, and her stunning indifference to financial matters, that her late father, and her indulgent husband, had left her financially independent, at least enough so to continue living in Manhattan to pursue her art full-time.

Emilie's apartment at 77 Columbia Street was in a respectable high-rise co-op, overlooking the East River. The Lower East Side neighborhood,

<16>

bordering Delancey Street and the Manhattan Bridge, was quite sinister at night. Yet poets came each Sunday evening, year-round, by cab, car, or subway, in everything from jeans to fur coats. One of the most bedraggled poets, Richard Bush Brown, was repeatedly mugged on his way home from Emilie's high-rise. All of us had what we imagined to be "close calls" on those nights, but we kept coming back.

The cast of characters at Emilie's readings was fascinating. There I met the phenomenal Barbara A. Holland, and most of the other New York poets I would later publish, including Donald Lev, Shirley Powell, Boria Sax, Joel Zeltzer, Claudia Dobkins-Dikinis, Boruk Glasgow, and John Burnett Payne.

The sad-sack poet-playwright Richard Davidson was omnipresent, always mooching a sandwich ("Could you spare a slice of bread? Oh, thank you. Some mustard on that would be nice. Would you happen to have a slice of cheese I could put on that? Ah. I see you have some leftover ham there. Could I put a little of that on my bread?...") Davidson and Glen shared a passion for the theater and she frequently accompanied him to plays. He got free tickets to many off-off Broadway productions in his capacity as drama reviewer for the *Daily World* (a Marxist newspaper which ironically never paid him a penny for his journalism). I would later direct and publish Davidson's verse play, *Song of Walt Whitman*.

Charlie Gould, a paper merchant's messenger with an unnerving resemblance to Joseph Stalin, doted on Emilie. He gifted her with a handsome pastel he had done, copying one of Doré's engravings from Dante's *Il Paradiso*. Gould broke with Emilie in fury after she depicted him in a poem, "To Let," revealing that he had taken in a teen runaway girl. He would later go off to live with the Hare Krishnas in West Virginia and came to believe that he had discovered the Ur-Language.

Gustav Davidson, an expert on the mythos of angels, and various officers of the Poetry Society of America, were often there, too, for Emilie was a longtime member of that august group. The PSA, with its headquarters at Gramercy Park, was the domain of effete versifiers and poetic dowagers. Emilie dragged me, squirming, to a couple of its meetings; as I was still in my rebellious Whitman-Ginsberg period, it was excruciating. She was forced to admit it was rather unseemly that the officers kept awarding themselves the group's monthly poetry prize. She resigned from the Poetry Society later when they opened their membership to anyone willing to pay dues. In her day, members had to be recommended, and pass muster with writing samples. Considering the sclerotic sonnetizing I heard at the PSA, Emilie must have been regarded there as a wild, modernist eccentric. Perhaps attending Emilie's readings was the closest some of these elder poets ever came to a den of Beatniks.

<17>

Poets, translators, scholars, students, and just plain lovers of poetry flocked to Emilie's salon, dominated by her fine baby grand piano. Some nights she would play her staples, her favorite being the Funeral March from Beethoven's A-Flat Piano Sonata. When I purchased my first harpsichord and gravitated away from the piano, Emilie was aghast. Bach and Scarlatti and Handel were fine and good, but how could you play Liszt on an instrument with no pedals? Fortunately for our musical accord, I remained just as devoted to the Romantics as to the Baroque. But when she came to my loft, she looked at my two-manual harpsichord rather as one would a basket with cobras in it.

The bad poetry at Emilie's was truly bad. Two of the worst poets in New York engaged in a poetic romance under our noses, sharing couplets like these before they eloped, married, and vanished (thank the gods!) from the poetry scene:

Tom Eagleton for Vice President ran,
But they said they needed a saner man.
Tom Eagleton really wanted to serve us,
    But they said he was too nervous.

For the most part, though, nights at Emilie's were a delight, and one could hear poems in all styles, translations read in the original and in English, and very lively discussions from many poetic perspectives. Bad poems were politely heard; good poems yielded fervent questioning. Best of all were the "world premieres" of poems written in direct response to a poem heard at Emilie's the week before.

When Emilie's folk-singing daughter Glenda married and gave birth to a child, the sudden death of the son-in-law (both alcoholic and epileptic), induced Emilie to make a drastic change in her living conditions: in 1979, she gave up the Columbia Street co-op, and sold her piano, to move into the brownstone tenement building at 77 Barrow Street to help her daughter care for her infant son, John.

Emilie took the apartment adjacent to Glenda's. It was dark, narrow, only two rooms. The toilet was in the hall. Emilie slept on a narrow bed next to the kitchen, and turned the living room into the best semblance she could of her old parlor. The Sunday night readings resumed. The terrifying night walk down Delancey Street was replaced by the welcoming streets of Cherry Lane and Barrow Street. Walking up five flights of stairs was a small price to pay for the poetic thrills that awaited one. The Village location also meant that poets could repair to a local coffeehouse after the reading was over, for more poetry talk and gossip. Such nights often went on until the cafes closed (the Bohemia we have now lost forever in the Yuppie-infested decades since).

<18>

In giving up her piano, Emilie had made the final break with her first Muse. She had trained as a concert pianist, and so long as there was a piano in the house, she was never really severed from that early promise. Now she would only play, with faltering memory, when she came upon a piano in a café or in someone's home. The piano would now become a ghost, its notes sounding but never dying in her later poems. I never heard Emilie complain about the appalling condition of her apartment, with its bathtub in the kitchen and decrepit stove and refrigerator: only the loss of the piano seemed to diminish her spirit.

Her Life

Emilie Carolyn Glen was older — by decades — than she wanted us to believe. When interviewed, she would terminate the conversation when the delicate question of age came up. In the 1977 *International Who's Who in Poetry*, Emilie listed her birth date as 1927. In a later directory, she revised that to read 1937[1]. Actually, Emilie was born around 1906, making her 63 years old when I first met her in 1969. Her birthday was March 13.

Early in her career, she worked for Macmillan Publishing Company and did a stint with Fairchild Publications — from what I can gather, as a reporter for *Women's Wear Daily*. In a poet biographical note in 1947, she indicates that she "covered fashion shows, visited wholesale houses, and saw child models at work.[2]" In this note, she says that her daughter Glenda was then seven years old.

Her university experience included a full course at Syracuse University. The sorority Alpha Phi Alpha lists her in the graduating class of 1928. Emilie continued to Columbia University and went on with her music studies with Ernest Hutchison at the Juilliard School.

At some point, literature took precedence over music. Emilie was not clear in her own mind why her career as a pianist ended, but the competitiveness and misogyny of the classical music field may have contributed. There were then only a handful of women among the premiere artists of the keyboard, and virtually no women in orchestras. In the literary world women, while embattled, could at least expect a modicum of success.

I suspect Emilie also realized that the choice between being a creative artist and a performing artist was one that had to be made. Many people could play Beethoven and Liszt; only Emilie could write Emilie's poems.

---

[1] Emilie was listed in *Who's Who in U.S. Writers, Editors and Poets*, 2nd edition 1988, and in successive editions through 1995-96. Her birth date there was listed as 1937! She was also listed in *Who's Who of American Women*, 2nd edition, 1961-62 and 1964-65. I would be grateful to receive photocopies or transcripts of these listings.

[2] *Epoch*, Cornell University, 1947.

<19>

During the 1940s, Emilie worked on the staff of *The New Yorker*. Only a single, brief notice, in 1942[3], credits her as a writer there, however. She may have worked for the publisher as a behind-the-scenes fact-checker. She related to me how *The New Yorker* checked every reference in every piece they published, even in poems. She recalled that a number of women hired by the magazine in the 1940s were let go at war's end when "the men came home."

Editing a Manhattan-based Congregational Church magazine appears to be Emilie's last paying job. Several sample copies were among Emilie's surviving papers.

During the 1940s, Emilie wrote as much prose as poetry, and had her stories published in *The Prairie Schooner* and H.L. Mencken's *American Mercury*. One story chosen by Mencken went on to be included in *Best American Short Stories*. Her fiction will be included in the second volume of this series.

Emilie showed me her long prose-poem published in 1953 in *New Directions*, but did not admit to publishing anything earlier. She had a slightly panicked expression, as I examined the book and noted its copyright date. "But you must have been a very young girl when this came out," I offered. Emilie beamed with delight, and we changed the subject.

The 1950s appear to be a fallow period for the poet. It is possible, though, that tear sheets and manuscripts from the 50s were lost, either in the move to the Columbia Street co-op from her apartment on East 15th Street, or in the calamitous later move to the tenement on Barrow Street. Researching and restoring Emilie's writings from the 1950s will be an important part of the work for the remaining volumes in this series.

The story of Emilie's marriage to, and her decades-long separation from, Charles Dash, remains a mystery to me. He was rumored to visit the Columbia Street co-op on weekends, although there was no sign of him at the Sunday night readings. Later we learned that he had been confined to an upstate veterans' hospital. Emilie did not speak of him to me, and her poetry deals with him only in an evasive manner until her later works (see *Dark of Earth* and *Rails Away*). Even in relating his death, as we shall see, the story Emilie told was not necessarily entirely her own.

---

[3] Russell Maloney, "Comment", *The New Yorker*, October 24, 1942, p. 11

<20>

The Coffeehouse Years

In the 1960s, the poet found herself a fixture in several Greenwich Village coffeehouses, where she read her poems and played piano. One of her few vitriolic poems of that period, an unpublished denunciation of a Flamenco-playing coffeehouse owner, suggests the bitterness of a failed love affair. In response to requests from patrons at the coffeehouses, starting in 1966, Emilie had little mimeographed chapbooks of her current poems run off and hand-stapled (*Coffeehouse Poems, Mad Hatter, Paint and Turpentine*, and others). The text of these pre-Poet's Press productions are included in this volume. I was unable to locate copies of three chapbooks, *Painted Door* (1967), *Just Because* (1970) and *Laughing Lute and Other Poems* (date unknown). If they come to light, I will include the poems in one of the later volumes in this series.

Emilie's 1969 chapbook, *Paint and Turpentine*, is a tightly-knit little poem cycle inspired by her friendship with Czech émigré painter Niko Mikeska (1903-?). It is a beautiful slice of the painters' Bohemia of Greenwich Village. Some of the poems are darkly shadowed by the political climate: the Russian invasion of Czechoslovakia the previous year disturbs Mikeska and shades her interpretation of some local high school student art anarchy.

During this period, Emilie collaborated with scholar Norma Crandall on a lecture-reading on the lives and works of the Brontë family. Crandall's psychological portrait of the Brontë sisters and brother Branwell was countered by Glen's reading of the poems of Emily Brontë, and her own poem, "Emily," about her literary namesake. I met Ms. Crandall on a few occasions, and lunching with the two of them was an interesting display of old school high society gossip, a time warp into the world of Edith Wharton.

Emilie performed in children's theater, most notably playing the Witch in productions of Hansel and Gretel. Stage-struck, she could not resist joining a small theater company on West 14th Street called Dramatis Personae, when they also offered her a Sunday afternoon poetry venue in their theater. Steven Baker, the director, had landed on the gimmick of staging plays with massive nudity, the audience members invited to shed their own clothes, dressed in just-legal "flimsies" as they watched over-endowed actors and actresses simulate Roman orgies, the sins of Sodom, Witches' Sabbaths and other sexual *tableaux vivants*. Emilie was the only clothed member of the cast, portraying priestesses, witches, or nuns. Her candid word-portraits of the actors and actresses in Dramatis Personae became the shockingly-titled chapbook *Twat Shot*.

The stint with Dramatis Personae ended when Baker decided that plays for gay audiences were more lucrative. He fired all the actresses and

<21>

successive productions were revues titled simply *Boys, Boys, Boys*. The theater later acquired a reputation for after-hours drinking and drugs.

Once Emilie was established at the Barrow Street address, she was able to attract a large and diverse group of poets and listeners to her weekly or twice-weekly salons (Sundays and Tuesdays). If she found a loft, atelier or theater space willing to host her, the Sunday events shifted to the other venue. Listed in *The Village Voice* and partially funded by grant money, Emilie attracted a big crowd and was able to pay her featured poets. The mix was eclectic, and one could hear a stodgy college professor followed by a longshoreman. Emilie fed everyone with juices and snacks, which the modest pass-the-hat donations scarcely covered.

Emilie was an avid bird-watcher, and for many years haunted Central Park with binoculars, a member of that elite society of The Rambles. Ornithology informs her poems, and even extends into one of her best pieces, "Up to Us Chickens," where she contemplates a feathered rebellion against chicken farming. I dubbed this poem "The Chicken Manifesto," and the hen became a symbol of our friendship. Each Christmas, I would search for some object to give her, either decorated with, or in the shape of, a hen.

Emilie's love for cats seemed to her non-contradictory, so long as the cats stayed indoors, the birds safely out. There were always cats in Emilie's apartment, an amalgam of hers and those left behind by her daughter. Hundreds of poems from her pen on animal topics found their way into print. Poems about birds and cats are, admittedly, rather easy to place, but Glen's best animal poems rise above the crowd of bourgeois robins and mewling kittens. Her other animal poems contain some powerful anti-hunting sentiments and border at times on animal rights issues. Glenda edited the chapbook, *Glenda's Ark*, which was subtitled *Mostly Cats (No Birds)*.

Although Emilie had not traveled abroad since childhood, she, like Thoreau, traveled much where she lived. Her bicycle was spotted in all boroughs, and she would even venture by subway and bicycle to Far Rockaway. She was a year-round swimmer, and swam with the Polar Bears Club. Her stamina was incredible, as was her resistance to doctors and medicine. Once, crossing a Village Street, Emilie and I were both thrown to the ground by a sudden and terrific wind. She picked herself up and resumed the walk as though nothing had happened. For days she sported an alarming lump on her forehead, but nothing would persuade her to visit a doctor or emergency room. I would have suspected her of a Christian Science upbringing, but I never heard a conventionally religious word from her. We both shared a gagging disdain for poets who came to her readings with little hymns and mini-sermons.

<22>

Emilie Glen As Poet

Casual visitors to Emilie's salons did not always get a consistent impression of the quality of her work. Emilie typically read off the top of her manuscript pile. Her listeners developed favorites, however, and she nearly always had her "warhorses" at hand. When she did featured readings elsewhere, they were typically a mix of "top of the work pile" selections along with poems from the published chapbooks. I think having the chapbooks served her well because they kept her focused on developing a reading repertory of her own best works.

Emilie would write three to half-a-dozen short poems around one idea or theme, and send them all off to magazines simultaneously. Longer, narrative poems — her very best productions — were one-of-a-kind creations.

Emilie's forte is the narrative poem. There is always a speaking voice, a character depicted, a story told. She freely crosses gender, race, and class, choosing outsiders, eccentrics, dreamers, losers. Some poems are character portraits, some miniature two- or three-voice plays, like the sad romance of the mail-room manager with the runaway girl who dotes on harps in "Hall of Harps."

Emilie seemingly had little interest in formal poems. She would listen politely as guest poets regaled us with pantoums, villanelles and sonnets. She was friendly with, and featured, Madeline Mason, creator of a renowned sonnet variant[4]. She certainly knew the classic poets, but her own poetry never imitated the past. Her technique was free verse, centered on anaphora (word repetition), rhythm, image, and a child-like sense of word play. Bursts of alliteration appear with childlike delight. It is a telegraphic style, a shorthand.

Her writings, often sparsely punctuated and with many levels of indentations, have a modernist "free verse" look about them, but only at first glance. Read aloud, her poems are completely coherent. Her orthography is a blueprint, just like a music score, for coherent oral interpretation. The extra spaces within lines are caesura, musical rests. Line breaks substitute for punctuation, yet suggest a modern "stream of consciousness" style.

I have taught workshops using Emilie's "Late to the Kitchen." This wonderful poem is a fantasy about a housewife who goes out to the ocean every afternoon, swimming, staying longer and longer, until her husband suspects she has a "beach boy lover." Finally she becomes a mermaid and leaves her domestic life behind. Any poet might have attempted this piece, but Emilie, like Jules Verne, researches the undersea world so that she can

---

4 A Mason sonnet is in iambic pentameter, with the following rhyme scheme: abc, abc, cbd, badda,

<23>

describe her incipient mermaid's experience in language of pinpoint beauty and scientific accuracy:

I swim across the continental shelf
　　　To a drop so deep
I have yet to pressure
Two miles down to the night of the sea floor,
The globigerina ooze of diatoms and radiolarian,
　　　And the dust of shooting stars:
I am discovering mountains and valleys,
　　Sea meadows blooming
　　　with lilies and anemones,
Sea palms　　sea grasses,
Whenever I like I can go down
　　　Into the dark red belly of a whale:
Fierce fish pass me by,
　　　I'm not their food and they're not mine,
I hear the sea creatures,
　　And they seem to note my bubbling voice:
Plankton　　always plankton,
　　I nibble on diatoms and sea lettuce,
　　　Nothing needs cooking in the sea

This excerpt demonstrates the subject research that went into Emilie's nature poetry. She was a voracious reader. Near her door always were two piles of library books, one heap on the way back, the other waiting to be devoured. Her daily reading was natural history, biography, history, science. She was omnivorous in her quest for knowledge about things and people.

Given Emilie's age and upbringing, readers and listeners were surprised at the Chaucerian, almost Petronian, range of her depictions. Living through the sexual explosions of the 1960s hurtled her into places the pampered little girl, summering in Paris before World War I, would never have anticipated. Emilie plays with sexuality and profanity, quite often turning on her discovery of some previously unutterable or unprintable word, phrase or practice. As our everyday language vulgarized, Emilie unbuttoned.

As a chronicler, she did not turn away from even the grisliest events. She writes about seeing a human head atop a garbage can; complains about the smell of her dead lover, rotting in a trunk in the closet; imagines choosing famous men to father her children, like Isadora Duncan; becomes a black boy who trains his Doberman to help commit muggings; plunges herself into a burning welfare hotel; contemplates becoming an assassin;

<24>

and perhaps the biggest stretch for her, inhabits the mind of a gay actor. She is impersonator, journalist, and humanist.

After I started up The Poet's Press in 1971, I quickly became Emilie Glen's publisher. Some of the chapbooks we did together went through multiple printings. Emilie typically chose the poems for a book, and I chose the order, sometimes asking for additional poems if I felt an imbalance in the content.

Our most ambitious project was the 1984 book, *Roast Swan*. This 67-poem volume, which went through several printings, was actually made up of eight separate "sets," each the equivalent of a small chapbook. I have included most of the poems here, retaining the section titles. Since most of the piano-related poems from "In B-Flat Minor" were re-used, to better effect, in *Glenda and Her Guitar, Emilie and Her Piano*, I retained only the single piano poem not in that collection. All told, seven poems from *Roast Swan* were removed since they were duplicated elsewhere in this volume.

The Daughter Poems

I invited Emilie and another friend to attend a gala performance of Mahler's *Resurrection* Symphony, scheduled for Easter Sunday 1983. Emilie arrived uncharacteristically late for our dinner at a French bistro near Carnegie Hall. She appeared distracted, but she was full of childlike wonder as we found our way to the fourth-row seats in the concert hall, with a very close view of the harp. Emilie read the program notes and said, darkly, "Resurrection, indeed." When we got to Barrow Street, she moved to get out of my friend's car, and thanked me for the concert, for helping her through a terrible day.

"What's wrong?" I asked.

"It's Glenda," she answered.

"What's happened?"

"The worst."

Glenda, a recovering alcoholic, had become addicted to over-the-counter cough medicines, and suffered an overdose. Although she needed to get into a detox situation, she was instead discharged from the St. Vincent Hospital emergency room and sent home. A few hours later, Glenda was dead.

Over the succeeding years, Glenda's death prompted a flood of new poems. Emilie wanted them all together in a book, but they were so unremittingly gloomy (and, what I could not say, so slanted in omitting her daughter's self-destructive behavior) that I could not picture a book of them, especially after we had done *Dark of Earth* and *Rails Away*, both funereal in tone. There was a real danger of Emilie typecasting herself as the "doom and gloom" poet.

<25>

Since Glenda had been a folksinger, I proposed instead a book titled *Glenda and Her Guitar, Emilie and Her Piano*, in which Emilie would counter the lament poems for Glenda with various poems she had written over the years about her childhood as a piano prodigy. The resulting book, published in 1991, was our last collaboration. I kept Emilie supplied with books to sell after that, but they were reprints, not new collections. I had moved to Providence, and I was not on hand to see Emilie's latest writings.

Emilie had amassed a large number of free-association poems based on "The Flying Spirit Pencil," a device she was perhaps using to break out of her familiar narrative mold. There is no extant manuscript of them, but they might only be pieced together from published sources, a project for Volume 3 of this series. As it stands there are just two of them in the present volume, from the 1986 chapbook, *A Dream of Amethyst*, edited by Michel Duncan Merle. I would like to thank Merle for stepping in to publish his own selection of her best poems, a limited edition book which he also illustrated.

I brought Emilie to Providence once to do a reading at the series I was running at my house on Transit Street. She came with her grandson and one of his schoolmates. We had a splendid visit and she charmed everyone with her reading; but it was evident that dementia was taking its toll. Friends in New York began taking an active interest in Emilie's welfare, most notably poet Vivanna Grell. Others who became aware that her finances had run out sent "care packages" of food. The poetry readings became chaotic as Emilie lost control of her scheduling, and sometimes two or even three poets would show up, each thinking him- or herself the featured reader.

Thanks to the inept management of her finances by her bankers, what had been a secure income from interest was turned into a charge account which Emilie and her grandson quickly exhausted: every time she ran up the credit card to the limit, her financial "advisor" sold off more stock. Finally, she was left nearly destitute, and as dementia set in, she could no longer find her way even a few blocks from her house without becoming hopelessly lost. Diagnosed with advanced Alzheimer's, she was committed to a nursing home. There, she gradually lost all interest in poetry, and in a final act of will, stopped taking food. She died on December 30, 1995.

<26>

Evading the Reaper

I can look back now over Emilie's body of poems and perceive how certain silences and evasions characterize her writing. Emilie the poet is frequently disembodied. She possesses the subject of her poem, but is seldom herself the subject. She invents and casts off personae, cannot be pinned down. And when she does delve into the autobiographical, she evades the reader still. Although Emilie describes the death of her daughter and son-in-law (both alcoholics), she whitewashes their responsibility for their own behavior.

Beyond this, Emilie conceals her own age in most of her poems about her young grandson, by refusing to denote herself as a grandmother. In poem after poem, young John is her *son*. This comes to a head in her ostensibly autobiographical long poem, *Rails Away*. Rail journeys up the Hudson, with the hypnotic mechanical noises of the moving train, pull her into overlapping memories, almost Woolfian, of a first love, then her soldier husband. The "son" who rides in the train with her as she brings her husband home from a VA hospital for his final days is actually John, her grandson. To sustain her evasion, she cancels her daughter. In her desperation to conceal her own age, she may also have changed World War II to the Korean War, but even this is insufficient to correct the anachronism of the "son," whose *Star Wars* toys throw even the invented chronology a-kilter.

Emilie's poems can be appreciated regardless of the underlying facts, and the majority of her poems are not autobiographical at all. I elaborate on these details here because I stand, as her friend and publisher, as one of the last persons able to put the pieces together while Emilie's memory is still fresh. Readers are curious to know when and whether a poet is writing her life story. Emilie wanted to mine her childhood for poems, but she did not want anyone to know she was born in 1906. Now we know the *why* of Emilie's perplexing evasions. An actress herself, the "younger" Emilie was her greatest performance, one she sustained with remarkable success.

The Emilie Glen I prefer to remember — Emilie as she was from the 1940s through the 1980s — was the poet's poet. Every writer who knew her stood in awe of her ability to work day after day, year after year, seemingly without a "block." Rejections that would throw other writers into a depression just rolled off her. She typed and mailed out a dozen or more poems every day. Each day's mail contained rejection slips, acceptances, tear sheets, printed magazines with her poems in them, and, once in a great while, a tiny check. On and on and on, for four decades she had done this, untiring, unremitting.

Working this hard, Emilie saw literally thousands of her poems published. Until the sorrows of her family life overcame her, she had the

<27>

privilege of being a full-time poet. She kept herself free of romantic entanglements, her mind free from cant and religion, and never touched alcohol or drugs. She knew exactly what the Muse required, and Nature had endowed her with prodigious health.

Well might we ask why Glen's work was never sought out by a major book publisher. Emilie was more widely published than many more famous poets, but she ran against the current of modernism. She concealed herself while revealing others in her narratives. She never seethed with rage, proposed revolution, traded in the threat of suicide, revealed lovers' secrets, or offered to solve the world's problems. Even confronted with death, she never saw a ghost or offered a prayer to invisible deities. She lived for the poem, for its making and its sharing, not for the "I" of the maker. The grief that shadows her late poetry — for brother, husband, daughter — never dims her quest for the beautiful word, the image, the moment. The pure life force that she carried comes through in the simple poem, "Enough," in which the gift of consciousness itself, of the everyday sensations of life in the city, suffices.

Reader, consider this: all the poems in this volume were written, so far as I know, after the poet had entered her sixth decade of life. What never-aging curiosity, what continual reinvention of narrative voice, what child-like quest for sense and order and beauty! Age hid its face; Time was deceived, and smiled; Death was deferred until the pen had been put down, the last "tone-stone" rolled uphill. Emilie's poems are her triumph over mortality.

As a New York personality and friend of poets, Emilie Glen was one of the happiest lights of Greenwich Village in what we now know to be its literary Indian Summer.

I do not know if critics will ever get around to Emilie's poetry, or whether they have already consigned her to a "midcentury" footnote. Emilie Glen's poetry is not addressed to critics and scarcely needs them. Her strength, and the key to the endurance of her work, is that she still believed in, and wrote for, the common reader. A posterity beyond us will decide if her choices were the better ones, as new readers discover her poetry. The publication of these volumes helps to mark her place, and it is an honor to do so.

I miss Emilie, my first friend in New York, and the first poet to welcome me to the larger community of poets.

—Brett Rutherford
Providence, January 18, 2009

<28>

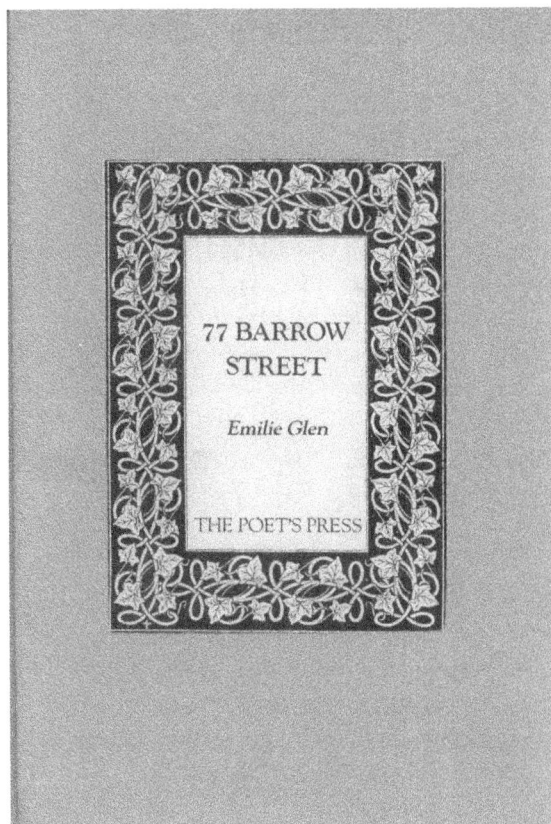

77 BARROW
STREET

Emilie Glen

THE POET'S PRESS

77 BARROW STREET (1984)

THAT PARTICULAR TREE

Father   I'm proud of you
  lawyer   judge   the Honorable
        truly honorable
Pride petaled into love
    when you told me about that particular tree
how you were afraid to walk past as a small boy
    on your way to the village at dusk
That tree was waiting to grab you
    snake roots crawling out above ground
    moans and mutterings from within the trunk
love you   Father   for fearing but passing
        that particular tree

WAITER PARIS STYLE

Croissants   croissants in the supermarket
      croissants in the quick-bake shop
new moon me back to breakfast in Paris
      when I was about eleven
tour party chattering
      a waiter tall and blond for a Frenchman
      passed the croissants
jolting forward in agonized alarm
when two croissants hooked together
      letting one tourist acquire two
Paris no longer a giving city
      city of lights   delights
Paris a scrooge city

Gazing up at the crescent moon
I'm still apt to see the horrified waiter of Paris
      trying to unhook the croissants
they come stuffed now
      with walnuts   almonds   raisins   cheese
I'm building a glass tower
        with an amber croissant atop

<30>

In the atrium restaurant below I will serve
        fortune cookie croissants hooked together
and if I find the agonized waiter
he will receive from "anonymous"
        hooked croissants flown in fresh
        from the Big Apple

OF THE NIGHT

In the watches
                the watches of the night
Why not listenings
                listenings of the night
creaks and snappings of an old house settling
startlement of windows
    in the teeth of wind lions
city that never
sleeps   a car starting up
        siren in crescendo
        late night typewriter
faint grumblings of an electric clock
traffic river beginning to flow
        neighbor coughing
        baby crying
in the listenings
        listenings of the night

<31>

HAIR IN THE WIND

My hair when I run
      When I bike
   When I stand in down-drafts from towers
Hair my red-grass hair
  Is a banner to the wind
The waves take my hair in mermaid floats

My hair folds me into sleep
   Keeps me warm in winter
      No need for a cap of wool
Ninety degree days I pile it up against sweat
   My Father balding even in his college pictures
I was his triumph of hair
   How red in the lamplight he would say
      Like Venetian glass

Curled to my waist in child days
   While I practiced the piano
      in early-morning snows
Mama would brush my hair round her finger
      To reluctant curl
One day she said I could cut it to fashion
   Ran home to hear Papa's praise
      But he was a thunderstorm

<32>

I tried to grow my curls back
   But they would flower only to my shoulders
Through the years I would tease him
   Now do you forgive me
He died without saying I forgive
   And now I guess he never will.
Hostess hair warm and welcoming
    Don't know the delight
       of taking it down from a coif
     For my love
It has never been coifed

My hair the flowering of my stalk
   I washed my hair by Loch Lomond
Waded out to dry it on a rock to dry
    Running my fingers through
       the red-grass tangles
     In the Scottish sun of my ancestors
   Papa watching from the balcony

<33>

FREDONIA FREDONIA

Fredonia
    walking past,
Hotel Fredonia   Welfare hotel
    of crime and misery,
I mist to the Fredonia of my growing,
    five going on six,
smell of the hardware store,
    the honey bun bakeshop
being stung by a bee as I reach for a flower,
    climbing the pear tree

Hotel of broken windows   rotting frames,
    crumbling mortar,
Allowed to go to a band concert
    in my nightgown and bare feet,
    sidewalk still warm with the sun:
Hotel close to collapse,
    Mama's parasol stretched shiny tight
    in our walk through tree shadows:
Fredonia
    Fredonia,
        so long

<34>

OUR PIERROT

"Only an animal"
ASPCA man mutters
    peering down the air shaft
"only an animal —
I'm not about to risk my life
    going down after a cat"
as if our black and white   our smudge face
    licorice on one side of his nose
as if our Pierrot with his conversational meows
    his leaps extraordinary
        fierce sense of turf
        eyes of jungle green
as if he is only a grease rag
Fire truck to the rescue
"Can't reach him   no way"
"Where are your ropes and ladders?"
"I'll go down on a rope," offers my little son
    "No   too dangerous"
"Can't you knock out a wall?"
    "Only to save a human life.
    This is an animal   only an animal"

Only an animal
We can hear our little cat meowing
    faint without pain
In the long silences we wonder
    Is he dying   Is he dead?

Lowering a basket of delicacies
    we hope Pierrot will climb in
    and let us pull him up
        but no

<35>

We ask the landlord to knock out some bricks
"It's only a cat   I can't disturb the wall
        when it's only a cat"
Frightening silence down the shaft
    "Dead for sure   it'll stink up the place."
Tears for his Pierrot run dirty rivulets
        down my little son's face
dissolving the landlord's disdain

"If you are willing to pay a licensed contractor
        to remove the necessary bricks
        you can reach your cat"

Two nights and two days
we call down comfort to his pale meows
Sufficiently paid   a contractor
        from the yellow pages
refrains from saying "only an animal"
        removes the basement bricks
            No Pierrot
                    no sound
        then scratchings

He is on the first floor
in the remains of the dumbwaiter
        that broke his fall
Takes no more than removing
        a couple of cinder blocks
        to reach his fur
Instead of letting us cradle him
he retreats deeper into his cave
    After our coaxing subsides to exhaustion
Pierrot steps out in all nonchalance

<36>

AS WAS

Asphalted Commerce Street
    curves country lane
once called Cherry Lane
    for its fragrance of cherry trees
Renamed Commerce Street
    the bronze plaque says on the bricks
when the Cherry Lane families
    fled the plague
Factory lofts were built
    to attract industry

Plague gone
    families came back
to the remaining turn-of-the-century house
    factory floors became artists' lofts
Commerce street still curving lane

This sunset
the plaque telling of the plague
    melted down in bronze flow
burning away the Commerce signs
    such a fragrance
we looked out of our windows
to a lane pinkwhite with cherry blossoms
    we'll be putting up signs again
reading Cherry   Cherry Lane

<37>

BLOCK PLANTING

Peach   peach   peach
the Block Association plants a peach tree
    in front of our brownstone
and I never went to a meeting

How will the newcomer's leaves
    turn this Autumn?
Golden like the gingko?
yellow of weeping willows?
    maple red?
Why, they're turning purplish pink
    like a feast of peaches
Tree in city celebration

<38>

SAYINGS

Come upon them now
  almost a year after my young daughter
    died on Easter Sunday
her child sayings
    penciled on scraps of paper
     casually put away
after all she would be a long time here
As every hair of her head is numbered
    so in death are her words
A four-year-old boast
    I know all about God — Episcopal
followed by I have a little sky in me
    and I love you with all my sky —
Night's pitch black   Milk's pitch white —
    Your little eyes are my puppies —
Ice cream cones taste like smothered flowers —
    My home is in your eyes —
Your spankings feel good
like a little rosebud being rubbed on my back —
  You can't have my comfortableness anymore
    No   no more

<39>

BLUE WITH DUSK

Skylight across
      Artist's skylight
A moon slide   snow walk
blue with dusk for my eyes to paint

Skylight across
    paints time
    windows the hour

Of course there may be no artist
    behind the skylight across
perhaps a computer salesman
a certified public accountant
   with a pocket full of pens
      Anyway   the skylight slanting
     in the slanting rain
reaches the artist in me

<40>

SADLY OUT OVER

Terror of lake,
Will it never leave me for minnows of light?
   Storm-dark lake
That choked out my brother's life,
   My strong-swimmer brother.
Mother's mother long dead
   Came to Mama before the waters closed over,
Looking sadly out across the lake
   Where we were rowing,
     My big brother and I

Terror of lake,
   My two-year-old runs off our Park path
     Into the woods,
Police   Park men   everyone searches,
   Worried over kidnapping   molestation,
He could fall from glacial rocks

Tufted in sun innocence   the lake,
Seeming harmless as its water lilies,
   It is I who find him,
Blue-sandaled feet close to the water's edge,
   My brother beside him,
     My mother's mother,
I storm down the hill to him,
   A small figure looking out on the lake

<41>

ABIDING

Tar paper roof across
    sloping roof blistering to many summers
Many rains to the tar paper roof   many snows
    rains budding   full blooming
       snows patterning

This snowless morning
    a five-point glitter on the tar paper roof
Order of the Star for being across from me
through many snows   many rains
    summer blistering

CAN'T CRY CAN'T SCREAM

Five floors of closed doors
closed doors down the stairs of our brownstone
    a baby crying full lunged
    child shouting
Behind most closed doors
    the silent ones not supposed
       to cry aloud
provided with no wailing wall
    only closed doors

<42>

MISS LILA

Miss Lila we call her
the porch lady on our block of brownstones
    Come see my garden
    from out her eighty-eight years
Up the steps into the dark hall
    ghosting a pier glass
past the sheraton sideboard in the dining-room
    the butter churner in the kitchen
    to the high porch above afghan blooms
white hair clipped cool easy
features for a flaxen child in a pinafore
    swinging a shiny new pail
    rusted now on the garden post

Was there ever a fountain
    where the impatiens bloom?
No a chunk of the city's old water pipe
Know me her message
    know me through my garden
    the house where I was born
    house I never left

Mama loved this garden clothesline and all
Papa little time for flowers
    working midnight till morning
    in wholesale fruits and vegetables

I went to business
  the typewriter they called me
a new machine not many could
    make sound like crickets
    five brothers and a sister in this house
baby of the family until there was no one left
    to call me baby
all here among these butterflies

<43>

Guess I always loved place more than people
being the baby of the family
        I used to listen to Letty
    see those four tires grown with bluebells
    they're from the Ford I once drove a bit
Letty tried to remove them and set out
    a row on row garden
    like people in their pews
the clotheslines   well I let her take them down
        providing she left the post
        where my pail hangs

ROUND AND ROUND THE RUINS

On our way   our hide-and-seek
        skipping way
    to the castled ruins of a comfort station
the two little boys and I stop off at derelict cars
    gemmed by smashed safety glass
they climb about the trashed wheel-less
    must keep cautioning Careful   careful

Running across the footbridge above traffic
they race the ramp to a Park by the river
    of tugboats and tankers
delay the castled ruins to tumble up
    a crackle storm of autumn leaf stacks
    their heads peeking up like gophers
        dirty leaves in their hair

On to the fabled comfort station
    of snake-crawl pipes and passage ways
    broken tiles in a room of wild bushes
shouts of discovery
    Careful   careful
bottles for the breaking to shivery sounds

<44>

They climb a window square
    calling me to see the one tiny flower
    a five-petaled bloom
        a minute alone
fight for footing along the charred boards
    crumbling masonry   twisted metals

Red maple leaves   locust seedpods
    all the delights
        of a burnt-out comfort station
Only in the lengthening sun rays
        toward an early dark
    are they willing to run home
    still in the glow
        of the ruined comfort station

A FILMING

Apples onions radishes   celery
    all because they're shooting a movie
        on our doorstep

vegetable cart from the eighties
    patient horse

Apples   celery onions   radishes
The street is not our own
    steps roped off
my little son must hide his big wheel
    no plastics then
traffic diverted   cars shooed
    air conditioners covered

Shooting over
we are offered a bushel basket
for collecting
apples onions radishes   celery

<45>

CAN NEVER

No piano
   no grand shining sunset
      my walks music remind
No room for an upright
   in a one-room apartment
   no room even for a spinet
On my way to the daily typewriter
   I tentacle my fingers
   as I pass the music school
      laddered with practice notes

Coming home to my piano-less
   I hear music minglings into twilight
      my fingers leave me
        for the keys up there

New piano in 2B
   a child at her scales
I climb up past
   The lid   the lid can never close

<46>

WAY OUT

If you lean out the window
     way out
you can see the river
     the Hudson
not quite well enough
with all the trucks and towers
     river almost to the sea
     salt tiding up to Albany
you can glimpse a boat
     seagulls white dotting
       a sail
night reflections spanning the two shores
The river can't pass you by
     if you lean out
       way out

PUBLIC

Leroy Street pool[5]
   beneath skyed gingkoes
   leaves garlanding down

We swim summer
   my small son and I
   his first strokes underwater
Leroy Street *Le Roi* King street
   Once Mayor Jimmy Walker's home
public pool intimate ours
   gingkos ours
   fuzzing breezes

---

[5] Leroy Street pool. A public swimming pool in Greenwich Village.

<47>

FIVE BROKENS

Here for the poetry reading
She stands at the door in the hat of fashion
    holding five broken eggs in a bowl
Is she planning to lay a poem egg
While holding a bowl of brokens
    The woman downstairs
Asked me to bring you the eggs her cat broke
    since you make omelettes all the time
Come in   Come in
I accept the poem
    of the five broken eggs

LADIES AND GENTLEMEN

Mama   look at that lady hanging out her wash
Mama Astor or was it Mama Vanderbilt
    Not a lady   son   a woman
    Ladies don't hang out their wash
    or even carry packages
Noel Coward's Dorrie had to tell her daughter
who complained the toilet paper
    was right down to a bit of cardboard
Ladies don't talk about such things
    Counseling my little son
I must tell him
    a gentleman never calls
    another young gentleman   shit head

<48>

LONG SECONDS

Just a second
    I sing out
        to my little one
Just a second   just a second
    long second
when he wants me to play star wars
or watch him blink his zany glasses
    long second
when he wants me to applaud
  his pink panther dance

Just a second eats pock-holes
    into the freshness of his find
If only I could spray them dead
all those seconds that roached off with our fun
    While you are yet child
let the dishes pile up   let the stitches wait
    the telephone go unanswered
Little boy   I don't want to lose you
    to years of seconds
until you are grown and not calling me anymore

<49>

GROWNUPS

No paper doll cutout
   my little son
set in a social page of flight suits
   and accessories
He has his own logic   his own games
   to tumble me out of my stance
Just now he circles the coffee table
saying I'm going to get a little dizzy
   then I'm petting the cat
round round dizzy round he reels
   toward the fur
   plopping down to pet
Why can't I fun into something like that
   Never wanted to grow up
because grownups just sit around
and talk and talk and talk and talk

<50>

MECHANIZED

Little one   why are you so grey
   so stiff in the joints
Surrounded by your space ships   your shoguns
   your talking robots
equipped with lasers   space guns
   swords of deadly light
you are silvering   you glow in the dark
   have sharp metal edges
Cut you don't bleed
   your voice beeps and cheeps
   tiny eyes winking red

Little one   little one
I can't cuddle you anymore
   I would cut my lips with a kiss
I must insert batteries
   check your wires
   play you like an electronic organ
Your name must be changed to something like
   MX   or Bazoler or Sky Jet
     my mechanized boy

ONLY HUMAN

Down   no I'm not down
   will be if I hear one more time
   the computers are down
   can't cash checks
   can't withdraw a dollar
The computers are down
   What do you mean, down?
If you mean broken   say broken
Do computers have moods
   four or five downs a week
   are getting us down
     down down down

<51>

RADIANCE

Down the aisles of our Church
Mrs. Spaulding walked in white
    ever since she lost her one son
    wore white in the triumph of trumpets

Child I was
    I looked up to her in wonder
    for her wearing of white
        shining white
    white containing all colors
Shall I wear white
        for my daughter

NAY DO NOT START

In our high meadow
  among wild phlox and bluebells
    discussion group it's called
the lady from out "cool Colorado"
    seeming delicate as dotted Swiss
stood up at coffee break
    and hurled a stoneware cup
    at her ex-lover's head
his blood purling from his brow
      like a mountain stream
  while he went to the hospital for stitches
and the hurler of the cup fled down the stairs
    in her red blouse and stockings
we picked up the sharp pieces
    of the fragmented flower
and did a show-must-go-on
    discussing the Brontës
Emily's "Listen I've known a burning heart
    to which my own was given,
      Nay not in passion   do not start".....

<52>

QUEST

Blood red beyond the mountain,
  Holy Grail crimsoning waters to the shoreless,

Golden Fleece illumining distant snows.
My quest   the perfect ice cream soda

Only soda I knew at six,
so bubbly tall I had to stand to the straw.
Teen sodas at the corner sweet shop,
    We would lean forward
          in our wire-heart chairs,
sipping through a single straw

Winters in the Manhattan of student
ice cream places are many as sea sparklets.
  Up a tower, the grand piano in tall tapers,
I am dwindled in concert class
  by all the prodigies,
keeping me from becoming a great virtuoso
  in the capitals of the world.
Still questing the perfect soda.
  I try a new sweet shop,
Whipped cream gives the soda a certain richness
  but toward the bottom of the glass, watery

Suppose it's an honor
  to become one of the master's assistants.
I sit in his box at Carnegie Hall,
  dine at his table
  teach his prodigies.
I marry one of the assistants
only to find he loves the boys.
  Almost find the perfect soda as Schraffts,
chocolate ice cream so petal smooth
  I almost forgive the seltzer sting,
  douse it with cream;
still no better than my glissandos

<53>

After concert class one April evening
where my prodigies performed beyond me,
   I walked into the Viennese
       famous Rumpelmayers[6]
real whipped cream that doesn't pfiff away,
   brings the soda close to perfection
except that the ice cream
      is inferior to Schraffts

Married another musician,
   a cellist;
Musicians must marry musicians
   or they have no language.

Managed to produce a son after six years.
No amount of trying   will bring either one of us
     to the concert stage,
those black and white piano keys
     have a baleful grin

My little boy and I go questing
     after the perfect soda,
     think we've found it at The Fountain,
an ice cream place in Macy's Toy Department,
no sweetheart chairs but a green-grey boy and girl
     under a rainy umbrella,

cool obbligato to much chattering
     in the room of mirrors
All I need to say is *more creamy than sting-y*,
     smooth as a Schubert song without words,
except that the chocolate syrup
     could be a bit more bittersweet

---

[6] Rumpelmayers. A famous ice cream parlor on Central Park South.

<54>

HERE'S A MOON

My son but lately talking
 Walks up to the yellow wall,
Picks me a moon I didn't see,
 And puts it into my hand,
Quick picks another moon off the wall,
 Another moon another another
Handing them to me,
 All the moons,
Picks so many so fast
 I have no more room in my apron

DAY WALKERS

Prostitutes in the day of daisies
 Turn quick lunch-hour tricks,
Two in a doorway swinging ready keys,
 Blonde with daisy-yellow hair,
 Redhead the red of devil's paintbrush:
If we rolled up the streets
  To a field of daisies,
 Would they run through the daisies,
  The cornflowers devil's paintbrush,
Roll and tumble in the sweet-smelling clover,
 Slide grasses to the bay-water,
  This day of daisy sun?

<55>

PICNIC

The moon broke into pieces
   and fell on our picnic plates
disturbing the starfish
   to a bitter taste
the moon was a melon
   none too juicy
we sprinkled cosmic dust on the sea anemones
   and called it a meal

STICKPIN

My Father's stickpin
   discreet diamond embedded in four pearls
Put away in a drawer along with rememberings
   until now   the fashion
ties and scarves cajoling tailored blouses
   I wear my Father's stickpin
   remembering the house on the hill
Saltines or petit fours left on the dining room table
   to say he was thinking of me on banquet nights
the quaggly duck he brought me
     from a business trip
   parades we watched from the window
   of his law office
   town clock when we visited
     the home of his childhood

Father driving us into the country
   to see the apple blossoms
   carving the roast at the long board
   of relatives
   taking pride in the scrawny grapes
     of his arbor
midget cukes knurly tomatoes
     to ripen on the sill
   Discreet diamond and four tiny pearls

<56>

STRIPPER

She pinwheels to our open poetry reading
    from the sex and nudie show
      where she strips nightly
    Coppelia[7] rouge-spots on her cheeks
    lids neon green
figure in the modesty of a Mexican
      wedding dress
    poems of her writing in talon hands

Timid reading as she is bold stripping
    her poems first tries at expressing
      the alone of a stripper's stage

She lights to our poem words
    as we would strip before her
but she must leave early for the late show
    the violets of her mind
    undetected by audience

---

[7] *Coppelia.* The dancing doll heroine (an automaton) in Leo Delibes' 1870 ballet of the same name. The story is based on stories by E.T.A. Hoffmann, and also featured in the Offenbach opera *Tales of Hoffmann.*

<57>

POW POW POW

Runs bird-foot   crab-foot   my little one
Taking off through the snow hills at the curb
    I smell my Mother
    I know she's up there
        Know she's back from the store

You mean you can smell her
        all the way down here?

I can smell her better in the snow
Snowflakes on my nose
        Pow pow pow

What does she smell like   your mother?

    Like wood   she smells like wood

HIS HONOR   THE SUN

Middle sized
        middle aged
ordinary middle sized   middle aged
        yellow dwarf
Just a minute   star expert   cosmic snob
        quit the put down
yellow dwarf indeed
sun worship about as old as solar system
No life without the God sun
        no time   no seasons   no us
If you can't talk in tones of worship
        at least speak respectfully
        of the almighty sun

<58>

SURE AIM

I'm the fish who spits at a spider
     spits at a spider
I'm the fish who spits at a spider

Who needs a brain
when I can leap out of the lake
and spit a spider off its twig
     into my mouth
Takes many a sure aim
even accounting for the double seeing
     of sun reflections
I can spit at a spider
     spit a spider into my mouth
Brain man   can you

<59>

NOTE THE HOLES

Spacing
   it's the spacing
      of the holes
so says the cheese commercial
   to the strains of Finlandia[8]
glorifying holes surrounded by cheese
   the spacing   the spacing of the holes
approved by the Finnish Quality Control board
   Do the Finns cut them out with scissors
   stamp them out with cookie cutters
nibble the cheese with patterned teeth marks
   Finlandia   Finlandia
we salute your planned spacings
   to the glory of cheese

Gourmet   that's what the cheese store is
  called CHEESE DELIGHT
  In fat cheese-gold letters
worthy of the billboard
  Swiss cheese sun rising over the Alps

Impossible to trade there anymore
Fending off the owner's passes
how can I concentrate on the rarities
  Danish Tybo   Cherry Walnut
  Fontina   Port du Salut
I'd rather enter a whale's belly
than put up with passes in the cheese store
  but Oh that mozzarella

---

8 *Finlandia.* Symphonic poem by Jan Sibelius.

<60>

HERE'S HOW

Out of child chaos
  I have grown to order
meaning the computer
still in our ordered office
  the computer is becoming too dictatorial
If I live by His Majesty's schedule
  how can I create?

Under computer threat
I'm letting my youngsters throw
  shiny scales in my eyes
I chase around without direction
  find treasures in the trash
everything useful a toy
  bathroom plunger to broom
we live in huge cartons
  dragged in from the street
poke holes in paper bags for masks
  children's disorder
  my order from now on
the deadly computer even tries
  to think for me
I'm told that by 1990 tiny silicon chips
  of little expense will be doing just that
    thinking for me beyond me

<61>

MY BACK TO THE GRAND CANAL

Venice sinking
   sinking into the sea
      long time sinking
I am sinking
   until I come in from
     the black swan glide down fetid canals
       past eroding palaces
         to the musty dark of a hotel parlor
exchanging a gondola for a piano
I sit with my back to the Grand Canal
   practice my scales and finger exercises
battle moth-eaten felts   dead keys
       broken pedals
as I did in the dark summer parlor
   of a farmhouse near the music school
no more sinking into the Venice sea

SNOW GIRL

Wondrous snowflakes
  each a palace of difference
Whitest white
   Snowflakes formed on dust points   ash points
     my young daughter's ashes
Chill comfort when I want the flakes
   to form a snow girl
   my daughter golden hair flying
   running into a cafe of songs
   down street from the Square of Washington
   opening her guitar case
and singing singing

<62>

ALL

Joncie beholding his first caterpillar
    lights up the heavens
lime green   fancy furred and feelered
    waveward
Artist   scientist
    he watches on the edge of all
    as we edge into his wonder

<63>

WITNESS CHAIR

Chair of justice
    Sunlit chair
Polished with much sitting
    Much rubbing of the arms
Curved to make truth comfortable
      The witness chair waits
         In truth for truth
Beneath the broad-long court windows
      That high the oak trees
         In a city of quick-rise towers
Long long window shade
      Holds down the truth
Great birding inside it inside the vasty room
      Judge's bench beneath the oaken canopy
         Places the truth just here
In the waiting for All rise
      Truth beyond courtroom face
         To earth eternity

Forest of silence for truth-listening
      Sun here   oaken here
As the oaken witness chair
      Turns morning sun
Into the golden brown of late afternoon
      Chair of justice
         Sunlit chair
You are truer empty
      Truer in oaken wait

<64>

MY DAUGHTER'S EYES

Eyes of forest dapplings
    A song to your eyes
      My folk singing daughter
    To your hazel eyes
Why long for my limited blue
    When your eyes are the hue
      Of whatever you wear
    Wherever you are
He who loves your eyes
      Loves many yous
Your eyes are blue
    They are golden
    They are green
Lemon lime in quick starting tears
    Root beer drops by the brook
Green in our green ocean
    Blue in a Caribbean cove
Golden in desert light
    Moist yellow-green of early Spring leaves

Autumn berries
    Summer bloom
Eyes ever seen anew
    Are they blue
    Are they green
Eyes of hazel
    Many hued as your folk songs
    Many hued as your moods
Why one hue one finite hue
  When you have the infinite in your eyes

<65>

OUT THERE

My friend the piano player,
   Pale handsome part of the seascape,
With his moon-pale hair and far blue eyes,
   Plays the stars down the dune,
Shakes off the drunks the lusting women,
    About his piano bar,
Starts up his motor scooter
    At three in the morning
   And speeds up the dune road
   To I don't know where

On night of stars fingering the wet sand,
   He tells me he goes up the dune road
    To land's end,
Believing this the logical place
   For a space-ship to put down,
He expects the interstellar travelers
   Before the sun dips oar into the sea,
Sits the dune beneath the thickets
   Of bayberry beach plum holly
   And waits:
Drowses sometimes like the disciples
   On the mount of olives,
Starting awake fearing he has
  missed the coming

My friend the piano player
   seems to disappear out over the sea
When he plays his own compositions
   Past midnight:

The dawn he fails to return
   We go to see if he has fallen asleep
    Into the afternoon,
Nowhere on land's end
   Nor his motor scooter
    Nor any part of his clothing

<66>

Nor does the sea give us a body
    that could be his,
      The coast guard abandons the search,
      His wife takes a lover,
And the unbelievers say
    he is just another man
    running out on his wife,
But going back and back to land's end
    I find bits of moon tinted glass
      In the beach plum,
I suppose unbelievers would identify
    as tektite
      Origin meteoric

MOON EMPTY

The greenhouse is going
    Greenhouse in the brownstone across
      Greenhouse lighted in the night
    Ferns golded
Young birches gold-greening
    Up to the slanting roof of glass

This winter-wind day
    Crates are stacked like cornstalks
The plants are leaving
    Spring of winter leaving
      Gone by dusk
The greenhouse flat with floor
      Moon-empty in the night

<67>

COMPLIMENTARY

Your Humble Servant
Your Humble and Obedient Servant
Your Most Humble Respectful and
    Obedient Servant
        Truly Obedient
    Devoted Faithful
Poor greats under court patronage
complimentary close to their letters
    often more of a production
        than their art
Fist shaking Beethoven
even he In Profound Admiration
    With Deepest Homage
    Expiring in Profoundest Submission

Before we smirk
How about our Sincerelies   Cordialies
    Trulies
    Very Truly Yours
Let's free the complimentary close
    down time
with Disrespectfully
    Tipsily
Your Exalted Better
Your Most Superior Master
    In Genuine Ill Will
Yours in Boredom   Grudgingly Yours
    In All Hate
Connivingly   Insolently
    or just plain Screw You

<68>

YACHT   WHOSE YACHT

So you bought the seagoing yacht
    the one with the teakwood decks
        brass and stainless chrome fittings
    the seagull upholstery
        flying bridge
We boarded your yacht at the boat show
        my little son and I
Our footprints pattern your purchase
    the hallmark of your fittings
My little boy took off his shoes
and cuddled into your queen-size bed
    your pointprow bunk
motioning me into cushioned ease
He opened drawers and doors and cabinets
    sat at your writing desk
        your dining table
    played star wars on the flying bridge
The sun rose that week
    only to shine on the boat show
    where the yacht was ours

By now the yacht purchasers must be
    out on summer seas
feeling the rockabye far away
    sighting dolphins   a blue whale
you must be feeling rather like strangers
        on your purchased yacht
    trying to luxuriate where
        we have been before you

<69>

Who's been sleeping in my bed?
    who's been sitting in my chair?
We're the ghost owners dropping anchor
        in distant harbors
Waking in the night to the ghosts of us
you must want to shout Give us back our yacht
    you but awkward bystanders
    Ours the possession

DAY THE

Day the geese
    white feathered victory
    escaped
        down by the East river
        under the overdrive
they cross nonchalantly against
        flustered traffic
stretch-necking goldfooting
        towards Broadway
Summoned bluecoats looking silly goose
        scratch puzzled heads
        over the insouciance
            of geese

<70>

NEVER FIND

My Mother went to mediums
    and she never found her son
drowned in long ago waters
    I traveled with her coast to coast
        waited outside the many doors
    but she never found her son

Never have I gone to a medium
    I look for my young daughter
in sun and cloud
    search for her down the street of noon
        in the surf I swim
    but I never find my daughter

SNOW ON MY JACKET

Snowing today
    six-point stars to the snow jacket
    my young daughter gave me last winter
particles of dust in the atmosphere
    form the snowflakes
the hexagons each one different
    in its sameness
    Could be ashes of my daughter
when I thought she would be with me
    a world of winters

<71>

NAMED EMILY

Named Emily, playing Emily
       Emily Brontë,
I swim the timeless sea
       to her heathered shore,
Climb the hill to the parsonage
not telling her I am from
   the Twentieth century
   where I breathe her to life stage nights,
Know better than to startle her
   with the terrible Twentieth.
   (Still the Twentieth could cure her TB.)
This too might alarm her
in her gathering of death like heather

     Emily offers me tea
at the table where the Brontës
   write of an evening,
The two of us sit in Emily shyness,
our words in leaf bracts on separate trees,
   I am keeping her from the moors,
   from the fires of her white page,

I would suggest we go out to the "lone green lane
   that leads directly to the moors"
only I can't let on how well I know her life,
her death on the very horse-hair sofa
    across from us

Ellen Nussey[9] says she plays the piano
   with brilliance and precision,
   I chord into Debussy,
   swiftly finger back to Bach
expecting her to sit down at the piano too,
but she has nothing to play to me   say to me,
I might as well be in the graveyard

---

[9] Ellen Nussey (1817-1897), a childhood friend of Charlotte Brontë, and a lifelong correspondent.

<72>

                    outside her window
Aunt Branwell[10] and her Father will be coming in
        any timeless minute,
Such a dark little parlor and she doesn't
            even bother
        to light the lamp,
I'll drink her tea
        and warm-swim back to my shore

HEIR TO A FORTUNE

Onnie's remembering me
    remembering in his will
Has to do with oranges
Met Onnie in my friend's hospital room
Because I brought him oranges neat of navel
        he named me one of his heirs

Onnie's will labyrinthine
    books so neglected
    no bookstore would be
    extinct stocks and bonds
moth and dust corrupting
    thieves breaking in to steal
    a nothing will

My canary diamond
    was supposed to be buried in clay
    and hidden in a beanpot
The executor found the beanpot
    broke the hardened clay
    to no diamond
so I go out and buy an orange
    in memoriam

---

[10] Elizabeth Branwell (1776-1842) was the sister of Maria, the Brontë sisters' late mother.

<73>

PIE WEDGE

Pie wedge
    this cafe table in the triangle
      of brick wall and glass
I come upon my love
   coffee cup pushed back
   from his work island
The pie wedge sun-rays another triangle
intersecting his Pierrot face half dark half light
    I move my chair close to his

When I leave he stays a while longer
    to finish his work
Never finished   always the editor
his unrimmed glasses crystals of second sight
Something I forgot to say
    I retrace to the cafe table
Away only minutes but the table is empty
    Always I will picture him here
at his pie wedge of brick wall and crystal
    in the come-go sun

<74>

HUNTER AND HUNTED

Birdwatchers' Edition

North with the south winds
    birds in Spring song
South with the north winds
    mostly autumn-songless
The Ramble in Central Park a bird motel
trees of tasty aphids down to the rowing lake

We hunt the flythroughs
    up rocks   down ravines
    in the underbrush
    about the weather tower
hunt the great and the small
    warblers in jewel tones
    black-crowned night heron
    scarlet tanagers
    an indigo bunting

Watch out bird watchers
    muggers flatten against rocks and bark
Beware the hooky players
    the gangs the loners
    out for cameras binoculars wallets

Our loot worth more to us than our wallets
    mourning warblers shy in the knotweed
    prothonotary[11] by the bow bridge
    kinglets flashing ruby crowns[12]
    among the viburnum
    oriole's nest horned owl snoozing
In the ramble of fly-throughs
    we're both hunters and hunted

---

[11] The Prothonotary Warbler, *Prothonotaria citrea*.
[12] The Ruby-Crowned Kinglet, *Regulus calendula*.

<75>

MAD HATTER (1968)

HALL BEDROOM BOY

Hall bedroom boy,
I'm a hall bedroom boy,
        Brownstone in the seventies,
    Actor making the rounds,
Sometimes in buskins,
Sometimes in thinning soles,
    Bachelor living off canape trays and buffets,
Rather a Boston-baked wit at dinner parties,
    Do an act with a ukulele

    Hall bedroom boy,
        A hall bedroom boy
On my way to glory,
I'll take any part,
    Any job between parts,
With my first Broadway role,
    All of five lines
        In a semi-hit show,
I start banking to take the flops

    Small role Desmond,
I act my way around
    Without being able to buskin my feet
        Into bigger parts,
Rent the adjoining living-room
    Which opens the door through to my bedroom,
        A suite,
I'm a feature player when it comes to investing,
    Some tweak at me that I should be in business

    Parts are scarcer
Now that I can only play the white hairs,
    I tried out my ukulele act
        In a couple of night spots,
But a ukulele out on rock and roll
    Is a butterfly out to sea,
Never let my equity card lapse

<78>

Even though I'm slipping from Broadway
　　To off　　even to off off,

　　By remaining a bachelor
I can afford to rent a bedroom and living-room
　　Above my bedroom and living-room,
　　　　A duplex
In the brownstone mansion where I started hall bedroom,
　　Of course the rent leaves little to spend,
My chafing-dish suppers are more or less meatless,
　　Can't complain,
How many who come to this cut-glass town,
　　Have gone from hall bedroom to duplex,
Practically an old mansion of my own

<79>

MAD HATTER

Litterers,
      Let's litter them
No litterer
      I go out to the unlittered bay of birds,
As many ducks as seeds in burpee's catalogue,
      Geese and even a whistling swan,
         Snowy egrets in the marsh grass,
      Black-birds rocking the reeds

Noons I sit on a log
      Juicing and crunching my lunch
I toss orange peels and apple cores
         Over my shoulder
      Like Henry the Eighth his chicken bones,
         Spit out the pulp
      Fruit for the birds,
      Bread crusts for the bunnies
The breeze takes my paper napkin,
      I discard my paper bag,
         Rain will return it to the soil

Noon on noon
      My litter hasn't blown into the bay,
         It tempts no wild life
      The rains couldn't cope,
Nature is quite a litterer
         I've been noticing
      With her leaves and fruits
      Her petals and pods,
Each noon I have to move down table
         From my mess
Like the mad hatter at his tea party,
Tomorrow I'll have to move right off the log

<80>

OVER WHATEVER

Say the words,
Say the words just here,
     Young man   youngish man,
  You're not saying them,
Why aren't you saying them?
    Driver of a bakery truck,
    Driver of a Volkswagen,
This street quarrel
    Happens to be over a parking space
      But there is a diamond point,
    There always is a diamond point
        Of reason
    Before clown-clumsy
      Anger goes into its act,
The crowd around
      Puts the purple in their rage
This time the driver of the Volkswagen
    And the driver of the bakery truck
Almost turn on the diamond point
      Of where each was wrong
    Before clowning on,
If they had,
    The youngish man
Might not be lying on the pavement
      Dead of a heart attack
As a third car slides into the empty space

<81>

PAPA'S MARKING CRAYON

Get that spaghetti off the stove,
      Papa would loud-voice Mama
         In the Broome Street days
    Of polenta   minestrone
         And cheeses from Bleecker,
Spaghetti tender as an aria
      He shouted off the stove
         For his particular pudding,
Marking crayons toward
      The buying of spaghetti

Odors of his burpling fluid
      Resined and waxed
         Through the spaghetti steam,
And I had to work this foot treadle,
      That windmill with weights,
         And glue on the labels
      Ponterio and Sons,
Sons   I was all his sons,
         His crayon-brewing sons

We would take our marking crayons
      Out to Washington Street,
Papa would laugh passersby into a sale,
      Caruso laughter,
And then was when the spaghetti cooked
      Until Get that spaghetti off the stove,
      Get it off for my markers

<82>

MY MENKE PLANT

Widows
    I mean the sod type,
This is for you,
    I'm watering my big-leafed plant
        On the fire-escape,
You'd find it in the Garden of Eden,
        Don't know its name,
          But it's very Tigris-Euphrates,
I'm watering my plant when sudden as a
        Fire siren
          I see it looks Jewish,
Drinking as from the brook of Eshkol,
        Mumbling none of my Yiddish,
          But pure Hebrew,
Why that plant is my late husband,
        It's Menke staying home nights,
Whispering love words fancy as my leaf-carved
        Wedding barn,
I can only tell him while he's in this
        Plant condition,
How I walloped a dame at a bargain counter
        For calling me a fucking Yid,
          And was almost hauled off in a paddy wagon,
Oh I tell Menke a lot of *gemutlicht* while I'm
    Watering him,
        Short of gefilte fish and knishes
He has the best of my care,
        I buy him plant food,
          Give him sun and shade,

<83>

And I water him,
   Careful not to cook his roots
      In the heat of the day
         Nor drown him with too much loving water,
The *yenta* think I'm a *mishugenah,*
You know   a mad one
When they hear me talking to my Menke
   on the fire escape,
But I tell 'em   *plotz*   drop dead

<84>

HAVANA BALCONY NOW

How is it beneath our balcony
    Our balcony in Havana
Now that we can no longer fly
    To its warm-stone white
Above the white surfing sea wall
    Does wash hang out pink white
      On the blue-red roofs of dawn
Does the girl in bursting-tight satin
    Come home before light
      Alone
Does the cafe man
    Call in his little brown dog at evening
Do the cab drivers sit at the curb
    Across
Where is the driver down there
    Who would rather be dead than communist
Do the people come to the sea wall of an evening
    Color the sea-pocked stone
      With bright shirts and skirts
Do the white carts bell rainbow refrescoes
    Is the fisherman's sky-painted shrine
      On the coral rocks below
A fishing boat lone-lighted into day
    El Morro   does it have new prisoners
Will we ever fly in again
    The sea curve is there
      The long melodic sea curve
    It is there

<85>

COFFEE HOUSE POEMS (1966)

GO GO

Everybody's watching her,
  Watching her,
Crowding this splotch of Broadway sidewalk
  To a fragment from New Year's Eve,
All but the boy
  Sitting a hydrant
   Under Times Square namelights,
His girl up there
  Shaking her fringed pelvis to a scrap,
Breasts danced down to little more than fringe,
  His go go girl,
   Go go going away from him,
Broadway's go go girl
  Dancing miles in one spot,
Come on inning with a shake a shake
  A shake shake shaking,
   Too fast to put salt on her tail,
Go go going up there with the steel band,
  Rapids where nobody can shoot a canoe,
Neoned fringe above where he sits
  Potato pale on a hydrant,
Go girl go go go go
  Go boy go

<88>

SUBPOENA

Prison is death at night
  Joliet is Black silence
  Black stone lily
Windowless wall
  Within windowless wall
A grave would be less silent
  In the seepage
What have I done
  Dreadful enough
   For deathcap silence
Wall within
  Windowless wall
I am stone weighted away from tree winds
  Spring singing ponds
A dog barking
  The bursting of seedpods
Insect voices many as stars
  No rattle bang garbage cans
   Not a car starting up
Nor an air conditioner
  Nor a helicopter bumping the sky
You know you've been put away
  Put away

Somewhere within stone
  A nightmare explodes the wall
   You catch onto a toilet flushing
    Hear your own beating fist
I subpoena silence
  But silence is always acquitted
For its crime in the night
  Against my person

<89>

FIFTY CENTS WORTH

Fifty cents worth, please,
Oh this is a super deli,
      Superest
Fifty cents worth of this and this and this,
    That shelf of sunlight,
       What's the price range?
How much for a balloon gone to sky?
     Fifty cents worth of clouds in the wind
An evening rock
    Holding the heat of the sun,
May I have a moment of that for a quarter?

     Snow   the way it drifts to diamond dust,
How much will fifty cents buy?
    Make it a dollar,
That field of insect fiddlers,
    It's for me,
How much to hear a hammer,
    Coal settling in the cellar
      To bumps and tinkles,
Siamese cat's double-tone meow,
    Swarthy smell of horses,
      Fifty cents worth,
Jumping joy,
    I'll take a spider web,
      The one with the dew drops,
I'll take the half moon plopped to the bay,
    I rather like skyscraper windows,
      Ten cents worth,

<90>

Oh and a big order of rain in my face,
      Bunches of bird song,
What about the shadow of that English elm
      Lake for my swim stroke,
          How much?
How much for the feel of satin?
      This deli is the superest,
To the best of my income
      I'm a spender.

<91>

JUST PASSING THROUGH

Just passing through slum street
     By bus or car or shoe leather,
People living in their own garbage
      Throw it at the passing through
        With their shut faces,
          Zoo stares,
Crash glass at tires,
     Hurl garbage lids
       Aim bricks through open windows

Every face a slum-lord to smash,
      Get even for rat bites,
        Twenty families to a stinking toilet,
Sewer sludge backing up in the sink,
      Bone chill,
Rip out the blood of the passing through,
      Bruise them black
Cops gunning through,
      Beat out their brains
        With their own night-sticks,
Grab their guns   kill cops,
      The footers smiling ahead
        To their own neighborhood,
The turtlers-in against the garbaged street,
      Holding their handbags in a death grip,
       Rob   rape,

The ones tight-roping between alleys and curb,
      Mug them blind-dead,
Give 'em the lousiest you got
      For passing through
        Just passing through.

<92>

WHEREVER THERE'S A BED

She sleeps
      Wherever there's a bed
Sheets   scratchy blankets   hay
      Floorboards with her coat shabbied about her
Runaway sea to sea
      Fifteen looking older with the hitch hiking miles
Hard new hair dye for every drudging stopover
      from LA to Manhattan
Runs from the percale sheets
      Of her pink ruffled room
Room roughed about
      By her mother's all night drinking parties
She'll be in the Atlantic Ocean
      If she runs anymore

Sleeps wherever there's a bed
      Kicked out of rooms she can't pay for
Fired   quitting ahead of police questioning
      A vagrant
Sitting up all night in coffee houses
      Sleeping in subways   hotel ladies' rooms
In restaurant kitchens by sneaking a key
      When men offer
        When she asks
She goes wherever there is a bed

<93>

TITS ASHINE

African belle in bronze,
  Tits ringing,
Out of jungle greens
  Into museum grey,
You have more lovers up North
  Than ever would be yours
    Among rain-forest blooms,
Your patina earths the green of jungle moonlight
  Only your tits shine sun
From the hand pats of school kids,
  Can't separate the men from the boys
    In the fondling of your tits
To the resplendent bronze
  You ask for,
Each new sun

SHOW WHAT YOU'VE GOT HONEY DOLL

 Scream scream scream,
Women scream my ulcers raw,
  Make me a star make me a star,
I'll make you a star, honey doll,
  I'll star you in crystal,
How would you like to pose for art glass?
  Excuse me the ever ringin' phone,
I have perpetual ringing in my ears,
  But it's for real,
What do you expect of me for a lousy ten percent?
  I can't build you a theater,
    String up your name in lights,
My name is up there,
 I'm Eddie the ulcer

  What's with you, honey doll?
Yes, the art glass,

<94>

You'd be posing for name artists,
Names carved right in the crystal along with you,
There's that ringing in my ears again,
Can't talk now,
Don't you scream at me,
My ulcer will scream right back,
A custody fight, honey doll,
No — no, not a child   our schnauzer,
Back to the art glass,
You want to wear what?
A swimsuit?
That's something of a shock,
Listen to your Uncle Eddie,

Nobody will know who's in the raw,
Only you will know   your secret thrill,
Every pulsing inch of your body carved in crystal
For class markets round the ever-lovin' world

My ex   she'd strip on the second Martini,
Used to streak out from the shower
Wet poodling her flamingo-dyed hair at my client,
I'm from the modest midwest, too,
But this is Reubens   Courbet,
Ever ringin' phone again,
Can't talk now, star face,
Meet me under the clock   four-ish,
Look   if you won't strip below,
Will you show your bazooms, honey doll?
Say you'll show your bazooms,
Do it for you Uncle Eddie,
Cream my ulcers,
That bitch bride of mine,
She'd flip 'em out for nothing,
You're getting paid,
You can make up to five hundred a week
Just by showing your bazooms

<95>

BUT ME

Everyone writes on the walls
    But me,
Legends of the ladies room,
    Ladies' rest room,
Restless scratches in earth brown paint, walls
    Everyone writes on the
        But me,
Among scratched identities,
    Four letter   five letter
Flushing of the world down the drain,
    Ladies wade through the overflow
        Of stopped-up toilets,
To scratch, lipstick, magic marker their say,
    Dryer floors   longer messages,
Handwriting on the wall
    From all God's people
    But me,
Must tell everybody how different I am,
    The world must know,
Everybody writes on the wall
    But me
        But me

<96>

PAINT AND TURPENTINE (1969)

PAINT AND TURPENTINE

Come   Come
        Come on
    Come on in
Come into my studio
        Riko[13] welcomes
    With the smell of paint and turpentine
In a swirl as of warm waters
        Swimming you inside
Finished and unfinished canvases
    Afloat on the rose-amber scent
        Of painturpentine
Toward seeing

CHILD HEAD

        Sketch of my child head,
I put it away with my toys,
        Child sketching child,
Yes I can find it for you, Cousin,
        Was I that sweet-serious
            In our Prague days
        Between the Nazis and the Russians?
No I don't want you to paint my portrait
        Now that I am grown
            And you are grown away from me,
You are across an ocean
        While I am left back here
Where our young burn themselves to death[14]
        In Wenceslaus Square,
Paint the Vltava[15], Riko,
        Only its waters flow the same,
Russian bullets scar the old city

[13] These poems center around the émigré Czech painter Riko Emerich Mikeska (1903-?)

[14] Czech student Jan Palach set himself on fire in 1968 to protest the Russian invasion of Czechoslovakia

[15] Vltava. The Moldau River, which flows through Prague.

<98>

And the new,
Don't paint the scarred buildings,
Don't go painting after the Praha you knew,
Don't paint me,
Monet never came back
Looking for his water lilies,

I fear your brush,
The eyes behind your brush,
Sail away on your paint seas,

When you painted me then
I was the one face,
Now there are paint seas of faces,
No don't paint me
Unless you can paint the face
Put away with the toys

RED LASTS

Red lasts
In the rain street
Lasts longest
From the explosion of paint pots
Out the windows of JHS 71
The kids hurled yellows and blues
That mixed to greens under tires
Hurled the purple of kings robes
Orange of fertility rites
Red lasts longest
In the rain street
Hate red

<99>

INTO PURPLING

Talk into the purpling of the pane
      Painter   composer
Brusher of paints
      Sprinkler of notes
Talk our two arts one
    Looking out on the forsythia office lights
Architectural ages in a coal scuttle
  From thinning   winter sun
    To grape-rich pane
Looking in on his canvases
    My music paper
      My notes coloring
    His canvases rhythming
Talk into the twilight
    The purpling of the pane

PAINT BURST

Happening
      Happening
  JHS   71
Art destructing
      Decreating
  Out the windows
Paint pots exploding
      Out the windows
Kids hurtling paint pots
  Who's to stop them
Nobody stops kids anymore
   Plastic pots hitting
     With enough force
To paint spray the wet asphalt
Seed pods bursting to rainbows
   Rocketing reds
    Royal blues
   Mixing yellows to lighted greens

<100>

The emerald city of Oz
Paint blops to pale Pollock
Fire painting across the road
Hurl power
Forcing the cars to paint too
With their patterning tires

Motion painting in the collage of hate pots
Violent painting that grows and grows
Solemnly regarded by passersby and students
Out to lunch
What happens
When the teacher
Sits them down to still-life

<101>

SQUARE GOTHIC

She walks medieval
Through corridors of paint and turpentine,
Always medieval,
Through seasons of corridors,
Costumed for classes seeing her gold glorious,
Her green velvet gown depthing to folds,
Silvering to light as leaves to rain wind,
Headdress ordered as plainsong,
Veiled to misting blue,
Angeling ice-clouds,
Steeples her fingers
To rose at her bosom

She steps cloistered
Among students rushing art down the halls,
Mounts the dais,
Her bones high Gothic
Above all the stretched canvases,
Troubadours of the brush before her tower,
Feeble the velvet, thicken the veil,
Square the skyward,
Seasons of canvases
To bins and trash cans, painted over,
Through galleries of paintings yet to hang,
The silvering of the green, the misting blue,
Gothic reach to the non-objective,
Rose in abstract

<102>

MIKESKA TO ISCHIA

Mikeska
        To Ischia
Words splash waterfall
        Mikeska to Ischia
I part the waters for meaning
Riko   Riko Mikeska
Is going to Ischia
        Island of Ischia
                Italian isle
Refugee from Prague
    His brush knew the cobblestone squares,
        The Vltava Hrdrcany castle
    People of its Parks
Off to the isle of Ischia
    To paint violet suns
        Bodies on a beach
Mikeska to Ischia
        Mikeska to Ischia
     Mikeska to Ischia

<103>

PUZZLING

Painter that I am
   I live in a paint pot
Fly by brush,
  Home into canvas
While exploring it into outer space~
   I'm not signing this
   As I sign my paintings,
You know my name
   If you go to avant garde galleries
You'll even find a couple of mine
   At the Guggenheim Museum,
Don't look for me among pop art   op art,
   Anything faddy
   Any one school,
Always I stand before a new canvas
   As before first stuff of creation,
Worlds within me seethe upheave,
  Now if all this is true,
And on my name as artist
   I swear it is,
Then why am I made an offer
   To have one of my paintings
   Turned into a jigsaw puzzle,
The deluxe kind   bit and round,
  But a jigsaw,

I who have confounded years of critics
   And gallery wise ones,
Is it proof of fame or notoriety?
   Anyhow I accept
That a child may know me,
   Putting me together

<104>

SKYLIGHT

Skylight a sundial
Each morning at eleven,
Light cat-walks the window rope
From panes above,
Sun's understudy hurtling to here,
Golden rope of nearly noon,
A circus aerial
To the flight of the artist

Reflection of a reflection
From a window unseen,
Light the painter paints by,
Sun candle in his sky window
Just at eleven,
Panes frosted to shadow bowls
Of blue and yellow roses,
His canvas sunned and blued

Skylight a square of heaven
Framing the picture to be,
Calling time each day
Morning light is best
Grasp the golden rope of now
To the flight of the skylight,
Great square
     demanding
       great picture

<105>

CHOICE

Painter's choice
    A tulip tree shakes leaf
Drops blossom outside his studio
    A lawn party of Japanese lanterns
In tints of green and orange
Tree his youngsters climb
    Tree to lean against
        Drinking the drinks of summer
Tree singing with birds
    Warblers' call notes like Seurat paint dots
A wood thrush sings from leafing heights
    This tree that roots in earth
        Toward heaven reach
It leafs against the rhythms of his canvases
    Disturbs his lake of light
        With its own hesitation waltz
The tulip tree takes his brush from his hand
    And paints its own tossings
He can cut down the tree
    Axe blow by axe blow
        Until he's cracking dead
Or he can let the tree
    The tulip tree
Take root in his canvases

<106>

GOODBYE GOODBYE

Into the twilight
    Goodbye   goodbye
Painter farewells painter

Art show[16]
    Bright spilling
Daubs the City Square
    Last day,
Crowds about the canvases
    Still thick as fruit flies

Goodbye   goodbye
From the flamingo
    In hues brighter than his paints,
The chin fringed   beard hanging,
    The seaman   the Gauguin strawed,
A painter something like self portrait,
Painters that can't be told from customers
    Except now in their goodbyes

LAST DAY   SLASH SALE
    Two for the price of one,
The unwanted   semi-wanted
    Canvases out into the world

Searching for a wall of home,
    The painters fold their camp stools,
One makes a last-minute sale,
They brown-wrap their paintings,

Cord ends enough to rope round the Square
    Are tied in separate knots,
The canvases are piled on carts and dollies,
    Packed into beat-up cars

---

[16] Probably the annual outdoor art show around Washington Square.

<107>

Into the darkening
     Goodbye   goodbye
Painter to painter to painter

Goodbye if I don't see you again,
Success   a good summer,
Maybe we'll get together,
See you next year
     Words like their paint-spilled leavings

Night of the Square is broken
     Like the scattering of snap the whip,
Great together   what apart?
Works beheld   words in full audience,
Praise loud as the clapping of hands,
Footsteps beating about the canvases,
From painters together, painters the center
     Back to painter alone.

<108>

DARK OF EARTH (1983)

RAVINE

Two apples
　　　　green apples
swinging from a branch
　　　　over a ravine
My love is being lowered
　　　　into the earth
yet I can only watch the apples
　　　　the green apples
　above the dark ravine

E.T.

Home　home
E.T. the extraterrestrial being
　　of the movies
My husband is wasting in his bed
　　at the VA hospital
I'm mixing him up　all six feet of him　with E.T.
E.T. in his little blue bathrobe
　opening his lipless little mouth
　　to a murmured　　Home Home

My husband says　　I can't go home
need constant monitoring
　　can never go home
He opens a parched mouth　almost lipless
　　to the cocoa I feed him through a straw
He took the desperate journey towards home
on a train down the Hudson
　　fighting for breath

Home　home　he mouths
　　his fading lungs lagging
Home　home
　　my terrestrial　extraterrestrial
　　　love

<110>

AND NOW THERE ARE TWO

Eight potatoes
    seven potatoes
and now there are six
    six potatoes
        five
and now there are four
four potatoes on the kitchen ledge
    waiting to be baked in butter
for my love in the hospital
    three potatoes
        two
After the funeral service
the darkness down below
    I come upon the two potatoes
    waiting on the kitchen ledge

BLUE AS

Blue as blue
    cornflowers in the grass
through years of visiting my love
    in the VA hospital

Cornflowers   blue as blue
this day of your lowering into the earth
    past the roots of cornflowers

<111>

SERVICE

Room service
   after a Roman candle night
hieroglyph drapes
   pleating open to city sun
red carnation rising from the white cloth
   carnation between my love and me
we lift the silver salvers
   to my waffles
   his omelet
pour the cream
melt the butter
     spread the marmalade

Room service   this morning
drapes open to the leafing trees
     room service for one
red carnation tall on the table
I lift the silver salver to waffles and bacon
   push the plate away
No room service down where he is
   down in the dark of earth

<112>

POPLAR

WOOD: SOLID POPLAR
   the funeral bill
solid as opposed to what?
   braided leaves?

Poplar   the tree of our terrace
before I ever met my husband
   poplar leaves would applaud
      my Moonlight Sonata
Lombardy poplars by the Inn
where my husband and I reserved
   a table above the lake
Lombards stiff fish
   compared to my wind welcoming
      poplar of home
always a dead one along the Lombardy row
mine always gave back moonlight
   to my Moonlight Sonata

Down there in darkest earth my husband
   wood   solid poplar

<113>

NOT GENTLE

Do not go
   oxygen tanks down the Hudson
   from the hills of his growing
     gentle
ambulance bringing oxygen
   before the indicator reds empty
   at Rochester Syracuse Albany Harmon
Will he make it to the New York VA hospital
   my husband
Do not go gentle
   no   not gentle
to go home again   home again
   into that good night

Back up the Hudson today
   without him
not gentle   no not gentle
Shape of hills gentled down from glacial days
   sailboats fireweed skyed woods
     horizon fields
seeming freedom of it all
   narrowed to a hospital bed
to be told you can't go home again
   can't leave constant monitoring
     never home again

Back to his funeral in the hills
oxygen stations in reverse
   Harmon Albany Syracuse Rochester
and we do not go gentle
   no not gentle
     into his goodnight

<114>

BOY WITH

Boy with baseball bat
Can almost see my husband in the black and white
   as the applecheeks of a long ago boy
   sturdy legs in knickers
     bat held strong
   eyes ready for the world

Years of VA hospital beds
   dependent on oxygen more oxygen more
   eyes clouding over

Husband mine
   swing back into the picture
   with your baseball bat

LONG AS LONG

    Charlie   Charlie
  I wish I had held your hand longer
You wanted it held for a seeming forever
knowing as I should have known
   you were going into your forever
Such an inviting hand
   sculpted fine yet strong
   holdable   but not forever
I kept letting go
Charlie   dear Charlie
  let me hold your hand tonight

<115>

NO SMOKING

Room of the immediate
    hospital respiratory
Nurse Nurse my lunch
    where's my lunch
I want my lunch
Quick Nurse quick
    more oxygen
    I can't breathe I can't breathe
Delirious I can't breathe
    need tomatoes to breathe
Cocoa give me my cocoa
Once blower of smoke rings
now in the blue vapors of inhalators
    in the room of the immediate
        immediate
            immediate

DEATH DARK

The train bringing me home
    from your burial
blacks out
    Now I know how
how dark it is this night
    down there

<116>

THE CROSSES AND THE VIRGIN

Years long
    evening pines
lawns sloping green empty
    to cars going by
      moon nights
Years long
    in a VA hospital bed
Today in the length of four o'clock
he sits sorting small crosses
   and miniature paintings
   of Murillo's Madonna
Bought them   from the gift wagon
to give to nurses   friends
   anyone who comes to his bedside
Who would like a cross
who the Murillo Madonna

I am nailed to the image
   of my love bending over the crosses
     and madonnas
       just before he died

HALF MAST

Why is the flag
   not half mast for you
     You gave all you had for your country
   not blood death in some green field
but slow
   above the green lawn
   of a VA hospital
   I lower the flag for you
   my husband

<117>

HOLDING HANDS

Seashell thing
        us   holding hands

Last holding of hands
     by his hospital bed
     a tangle of green tubing
He hangs on   hangs on
     when it is time to let go

IS ARE HAS

Your crossword puzzle books
   my husband
months of books
from your VA hospital bed
   Back home without you
the much used   the never used
My list of the books you had   had wanted
   Past tense closes over you
Hereafter I shall use only the present
   present tense

<118>

BELONGINGS

Clutter in the hospital bed stand
   when you want only what you are looking for
My love wants a spoon the cocoa mix
Now Now every need Now
   Now all he is
breathing oxygen through a tube
   into lungs almost gone
Everything life life and death

   Now Now
His belongings something to mess through
   until today
Back in the home he will never re-enter
   each thing precious even sacred
   crystalled with my tears
his crossword puzzles
pajamas too large for his wasting
   razor old spice

the cushion I selected of the right firmness
   I hug it to me
as I couldn't hug him tangled
   in green and yellow tubing
   letters from me no meaning now
the star sapphire ring I gave him
   crystalled with the most tears
     his sapphire ring

<119>

WITH A SHOUT

He got me there
my husband got me there
   got me to the sea
shouted at me like the drill Sergeant he was
   but he got me to the sea
rose copper into moonlight swims
   under the summer triangle
   Altair   Deneb   Vega
to the Inn on the dunes
where I could run down beach stairs
   into the surf

Quiet now   too quiet about the house
   death quiet
gone on without me
   where
earth dark below
   or skies beyond the summer triangle

<120>

LATE TO THE KITCHEN (1976)

HOW THEY COME

See how they come
See how they come
    How they come
  To the door of poetry
See how they come
  To the open reading
One stands at the door
    With a motorcycle helmet
      Under his arm
A girl plucks her poems
    From out her white muff
Paintings under the arm
    Poems in his hand
      He waits at the door
The four stand their height
    Like a basket-ball team
Barefoot she comes
    He in muddy boots
Mica dust twinkling his work clothes
    They are at the door
With duffel bags   rope-tied suitcases
In a wheel-chair   on crutches
With a folding bike   a bongo drum
    A pet raccoon
Poems typed
    Poems scrawled   scratched
      In notebooks   portfolios
    Dispatch cases   scraps of paper

<122>

She stands at the door
    Working her arms out of her snow coat
Poems between her teeth like a puppy
    See how they come
        See how they come
    How they come
        How they come
    How they come
            Come
Come

<123>

DEATH'S HOTEL

Yesterday's rain
Down through the remains
   Dismaling down
Yesterday's rain
   Through the wreckage
     Of yesterday's hotel
The old Broadway Central[17] fallen of age
   Hotel once faceting
Jim Brady's diamonds among prismed chandeliers
   Now death's hotel
Hotel of welfare caseloads
   Collapsed under the weight of misery
Ambulances for the dying have sirened off
   New pine boxes for the dead removed
Crane gone   fire engines   police cars
   No more turret lights   spot beams
     Only the street-lamp dark
As the remains wait for whatever
   Is to be done
Rain belated inspector of the walls
   Rain doing the digging
Down to the cluttered pit of death
   Yesterday's rain in a variety of strums
Gurgling   burpling   cascading
   Drip   drip   dripping

   Down wrecked stories
Allegro   adagio
    Raindrop postlude
   Through bricks and plaster and rotting wood
Wet earth the smell of a thousand
   Decaying mushrooms
Yesterday's rain
   Down the tottering cornices

---

[17] The Broadway Central, on Broadway at Bleecker Street, was built in 1870, and was once the largest hotel in the world. Decayed into a flophouse called The University Hotel, it collapsed in 1973.

<124>

           No exit   exit signs
        Banging doors   upended floors
        Crutches   furniture   beat icebox
             Cracked mirrors
Rain in final statement

SO I

And so I opened
      My apartment door
   To the ringing of bells
Bolted myself in
And said Merry Christmas
To the cats

<125>

BERRY BRIGHTS

Where there's a berry
    There's a way
Where there's a way
    There's a berry
Where there are birds
    There are berries
      Berry-eyed birds at the berries
Greener the berry   farther the bird
    Berries in the cream light
    Berries in the bowl
Berries too bright for the fresh-carved grave-stone
    Berries startling the bay walk
Berries in a basket
Berries in a box
   Which came first   the berry or the mouth
A berry   a berry   popberries of the sea
   Bacchus berries flying the birds upside down
Berry down dizzy
   Up down dizzy
   Down dizzy

<126>

PAINTED OUT

Painted out,
   The woman who died in the night,
Painted out as if she had never been,
    Sun-cream paint glistening on the first
       floor front
           Door hanging open,
She would be sitting in the lamplight,
   Cat furring the sill,
When I climbed the brownstone steps,
   Long shadows into velour depths,
Mysteries of the mantelpiece,
   Mirror blue glinting,
Castle candle in brown-red glow

Sun-cream paint,
   And the door hanging open,
The place small empty
   Now she is painted out,
The clear-browed woman,
   Hair in sober coif,

Painted out in a glister of sun-cream,
   Her belongings a pile of trash
     Under her once window,
Painted out as if she had never been

<127>

ISADORA HAD IT FIGURED

If Isadora[18]
      I can
  Dance
      To her eugenics
Choose great Fathers
     One per child
   First born must be musical
Fathered by Leonard Bernstein or
     Julian Bream.

   Not being Isadora
I must mate with a dancer
     To achieve a dancer
   Nureyev
If he would be willing to function
   Edwin Way Teal   the naturalist
   How old is he   anyway
Physicist   no thank you
   Statesman
        Are there any

Lindsay[19] for looks
  I must have Lindsay
     No matter what he produces
Actor
  I might sample more than one
Pinter the playwright
    He's around   isn't he

---

[18] Isadora Duncan, a founder of modern dance, refused to marry any of her lovers.

[19] John Lindsay (1921-2000) the popular Mayor of New York City from 1966 to 1973.

<128>

Louis Nizer [20]   Nader   Udall[21]
    Fellini   Yevtushenko

  Financier
My young will need one
    Not Howard Hughes   nor Hugh Heffner
        This requires more research
I'd like a go at Billy Graham
    Return engagement whenever the results warrant
One muscle boy
    I'll have to bone up on sports
Toothsome as I am
    Who says they'll all say Yes
        A wife or so might object
I must have a secondary   tertiary list at least
Maybe I should just marry Marty

---

[20] Louis Nizer (1902-1994), celebrity lawyer and philanthropist, in his time the highest-paid lawyer in the world.
[21] Stewart Udall (1920-), Secretary of the Interior in the Kennedy and Johnson administrations, a hero to environmentalists as the savior of the New Jersey Great Swamp, a haven for migratng birds.

<129>

LATE TO THE KITCHEN

My husband purples
      When I'm late preparing his dinner,
Each night I'm at the stove later,
   He fears I have an afternoon lover,
A lover is not what I have,
      But love,
    A love powerful of voice,
A love from the beginning of globe time,
   A zillionaire handsome beyond men;
The sea is my love,
   Its rhythming waves,
Tugging   tossing   seething   rocking,
Waters sec   waters mellow
Satin ribbon waters   sparklers

I am late to the kitchen
   For swimming the glory sea,
And I'm learning how to stay under longer
   Without a snorkel,
The air spaces are there for my finding,
   And I'm developing my rudimentary gills:
Each day I swim out farther,
    Come to the kitchen later,
  The sea wants me,
I swim across the continental shelf
     To a drop so deep
I have yet to pressure
Two miles down to the night of the sea floor,
The globigerina ooze of diatoms and radiolarian,
    And the dust of shooting stars:

<130>

I am discovering mountains and valleys,
   Sea meadows blooming
      with lilies and anemones,
Sea palms   sea grasses,
Whenever I like I can go down
      Into the dark red belly of a whale:
Fierce fish pass me by,
      I'm not their food and they're not mine,
I hear the sea creatures,
   And they seem to note my bubbling voice:
Plankton   always plankton,
  I nibble on diatoms and sea lettuce,
     Nothing needs cooking in the sea

My husband complains I taste like a salt stick;
     Am cold to the touch;
   Smell like a fish market:
Track kelp and seaweed around the kitchen,
   And scatter sand in the bed:
He still suspects I have a beachboy lover
      When I'm building a blue pearl grotto
      Out among the anemones:
When I'm beginning to pressure down
    To the neon'd night
Of fish with lighted portholes like ships,
   Fish carrying lanterns on their heads:

When I swim to the sun-green upper waters
      To fly with the flying fish,
    Ride the backs of dolphins,
I snap the hooks of fishermen,
     Rip their nets,
   Bend harpoons and marlin spikes:

<131>

Mermaid that I now am
    I surface to a rock island,
My sea-green hair about my breasts,
      A rainbow sea pearl hanging from my forehead
      By a strand of kelp;
My sea collar is crimsoned with algae:
      I confound sailors as I sit
        Waving a sea fan:
My husband may come upon me one day,
    And be troubled by the resemblance
To a wife who came late to the kitchen,
      As I slide off the rock
        Into the sea

LOST

The lost Atlantis
      May not be lost
        Down there
We may be lost
      Up here

<132>

MAN

No man
    Is
        An island
    Is
        An island
    Is
        Man

SHAPE OF A GRAND

World   a grand
   Lid lifted
      Triangled
  Dark polished
Shaking off the globe
     In its mahogany thrust to the skies
Pedals deep into the earth of resonance
     Mighty pianoforte
Alpine keys to an Everest of tone
     Black forest of sharps and flats
Grand   great grand
     For my tone-tipped fingers
Grand in the wind of hurricane
     Pianissimo of rain-drops on birch leaves
Rack for world music
     Earth the great shape of a grand piano

<133>

WHICH CAME FIRST

Which came first
   My little son has found a way
      Out of his high crib
         Came first
Found how to open the icebox door
        Which
Pressed me awake with an egg in my hand
       Came first
Left a buttercup meadow of broken eggs
      Behind his running
     To wake me with an egg
       Unbroken.

BOBBING BENEATH

Pumpkin heads
   Bobbing beneath me
My head up here brook clear
   Their tops in candle flame
Smell of the scorched flesh of pumpkins
   If I am not careful I'll be singed
Which means I must beat off the pumpkin heads
   Send them rolling down the hill
So I can breathe up here

<134>

STRING

String hanging from a hole in the plaster
   String a little dirty
   Plaster white as
I pull at the string
   Which pulls down long   long
      Longer
A big ball's worth   a kite's worth
     Hole black through
       To the other side
I knock at the door next mine
     A woman answers
Says I don't know what you mean
    There is no hole in my wall
I keep pulling   pulling   pulling
   And there is no end to it
     The string

HIS INDOOR WIFE

Her husband returns to her
   Now she is dead,
Her true lover husband,
   True love of sea,
Comes to a wife no closer
   To his sea
Than the salt in her cooking water,
   Returns ordering cremation
     With burial at sea,
   The seaman's service,
He scatters her ashes
   Upon the salt-sea waters
Making her his own

<135>

BAY WALK

Can it still be there
       The bay walk?
How can it still be there
       Now I've left
Snowy egrets across the browning marshes,
The bay sparkling about the ducks,
Speckle-berry branches of Russian olive
     Bending low over my head,
Gold-crowned kinglets among the pines
Cedar waxwings in the cedars,
Rose-hips and beach rose all on one bush;
     I smelled a camphor flower,
      Mock orange and Mexican tea,
If I don't hear it   see it   smell it   taste it,
     Can the bay walk be there?
Not possibly
     Now I've left

TIPPED

Orange cat on my back
   Wakes me to a fragrance
      Not particularly cat
Why his whiskers are tipped orange pink
   He has grown rosebuds in the night
If my cat can
    I can
   Grow rosebuds at hair tip
In the dream state   I suppose
   It will take delicate vibrations
     Between me and cosmos
   For me to waken with rosebuds
Then my cat and I will sit around
   On cushions
Much sought after
   For our rosebud tips

<136>

EMILY

Emily[22]
   Of the moors
I am Emilie,
You are Emily,
   I walk the shore
And my steps are yours.
    We walk into the blue violet distance,
You across purple heather,
I across golden sands,
   Yours the moor winds,
   Mine the sea winds.
I am of the world
   But not of the world,
Your are not of the world
   But of the world.
I who lost my brother when I was six,
   Lost him by drowning,
    Yet I walk the sea,
Wonder how it was with you and your brother
    Across moors wilder
  Than the sea I walk.
In the waves I hear many voices,
    Hear his,
In the moor winds you hear one voice.
As long as I walk,
   You walk,
Walk heather to the sea

---

22 Emily: Emily Brontë, poet and author of *Wuthering Heights*.

<137>

UP TO US CHICKENS

EMILIE GLEN

UP TO US CHICKENS (1972)

HELLO

All winter away
    Thrushes   tender thrushes
Their spots spotting May
I missed them all winter
  But they never missed me

Myrtle warblers
Rain scrubbed
But not for me
Yellow patching
Among the forsythia
They don't care I waited for them
    All winter
Any bug on the bark
Has a better welcome

The Northern water-thrush
    Doesn't go about fine striping
That I'm here to say Hello

Not a returning bird
Cares that I waited all winter

<140>

EVER

See you
My son walks away from me
In his tallness   blondness
Swimmer's figure
Stroking through waves of shadow leaves
My eyes chase after him

See you
Two way sun ray
Taking him to class
My student son
Who will be building tomorrow's bridges
If that is what he wants
    Light footing me into a supermarket
After the family's favorite dishes

See you
His last words
See you
Last time ever
A car jumped the curb
Crushed him against the wall
My son
See you

<141>

DID YOU HEAR ABOUT JENNY

Jenny   say Jenny   say Jenny,
A Mother who names her daughter Jenny
Wants for her a sweet-grass life:
When someone asks Did you hear about Jenny?
All the Jenny wrens
Come out from rock hollows of the mind

This Jenny
Wears her name like a jacket
Left over from high-school:
Such a pale Jenny,
Dark eyes taking up most of her face,
In her first stage role
So at home in the dying scene
That the audience almost did a double take
When she came up out of death
To bow

Jenny   day-named Jenny
Child of the moonless night,
Named Jenny   home Jenny
By a Mother who wanted her daughter
To bake   to sew   to sun   to live:

What about Jenny? What happened to Jenny?
She died for real,
Took her own life,
Jenny ran after death along the bank
Of dark flowers,
Jenny   Jenny
We say her name   say her name
Call after Jenny   Jenny wren

<142>

PINK TO THE GUTTER

Blood on the sidewalk
   Rain washes the blood
On the sidewalk
Flows it pink to the gutter
   Where the child
      Sails a paper boat

OFF HAND

Off hand
You're on a disaster course
Off hand
I don't believe you'll ever make it
Off hand
It can only end in divorce
Off hand
Off hand
I question your talent
Off hand
We're through
Off hand
Off hand

Oh by the way
Drop dead

<143>

DOBIE

Dobie   I call my dog
On account of he's a Doberman pinscher,
I've had him since he was a puppy,
My brother found him lost in the Park
Just before he was cooped for armed robbery:
We trained him to guard our place
    From junkie thieves,
I ain't no junkie at thirteen
Like some in my class,
But I gotta steal from honkies
On account of they made slaves of us blacks;
I spend my loot on Ma and my sisters,
Tell 'em I have a job nights scoopin' ice cream.
If honkie don't give me no money
I say to Dobie   Rip him
And the guy comes across quick

Man and his horse,
How it was in the old West,
In this jungle town it's man and his dog:
Dobie is black like me
Except he has brown eyebrows
And brown under the chin
Like I have pink heels and palms;
He licks my face like a lollipop,
Looks up at me from under them brown
    eyebrow spots,
Jumps me with a lotta love,

Plenty of dog   Dobie,
Plenty of dog   all mine,
And I'm all his
Right now I'm in youths' detention,
This guy wouldn't give up his wallet;
I said to Dobie   Rip him.
When that didn't work I let him off the leash,
    And did he rip,

<144>

Bloodied him all over
While I went through his pockets,
One of them unmarked cars spotted me:
Dobie and I ran into the park,
When I see we're cut off
I say to Dobie   Rip him
But when I see they're gonna shoot him
I say   Heel   Dobie   Heel

So here I am in detention without Dobie,
    But he's jumpin' and barkin'
And playin' with the red rubber bone
        I stole off a pet shop
On account of we have it comin' to us

<145>

NAKED ROUND

Round round the round
She paces
The girl from Iran
Fierce of face
Heavy breasted
Clothed only in her hair
Black snaking
Round round the round
In the foyer of the theater in the round
Lunging like a yak
From the stage round
Where she sits odalisque
While the Sodomites orgy beneath
   She paces round round the round
Naked round like a hostile tribe
The girl from Iran
Round round   naked round
Her mind done up in many petticoats

<146>

BALD

I lay down bald
I in my twenties
And no Yul Brunner
Lay down bald
In a summer field
Woke to a feeling of growth
Through my scalp
Flowers
I was growing a head of flowers
Tangle of moon blooms
Reluctantly
I had a barber cut my flower hair
But the moon flowers are growing again
Even more luxuriant
In the fragrance of woods after rain
For the delectation of women
Glory of my mirror

<147>

UP TO US CHICKENS

Chicken that I am,
White of feather,
A leghorn,
Descended from the jungle flyers
    Of India
I can see we're nothing but egg machines
    In the third-degree glare
Of our well-kept coops
Laying eggs   white eggs
White eggs   white eggs

Slick feel,
Eggs rolling out of me,
Like eating in reverse,
But they're always being grabbed
Out from under my warming feathers

Sometimes I just can't lay,
I roost wondering how it was
    With jungle flyers,
I can flutter flap about the yard,
But we chickens laze around
On over-rich food too easy to come by.
What poor wingers we are,
Flap flap   flutter flap,
While birds small enough
To tuck under our wing,
Fly over our heads

Separating myself from the others
    I go off into the woods,
And flex my wing muscles,
Exercise them until they ache
Toward the flight of our ancestors
When white flocks flew over the jungles,
Over cane brakes and bamboo thickets

<148>

I may not be an eagle
But I will learn to fly
As well as a finch,
When I'm with the others,
I keep it a secret,
The new strength of my wings

With the Spring South wind
I rise on a spiral of warm air
    To the height of warblers
Flying North,
I a flutter-flap chicken
    In full flight,
I sleep in the night
Instead of laying eggs to light bulbs,
Sit only the eggs I choose to lay
Warming them to new birds for flight,
And I will return with the North wind
To teach the flocks how to fly,
Wild free

<149>

NEW BUST

New bust in the cast
Le Sacre du Printemps[23]

New bust in the cast
   New nude

Just when our dancers have flopped
   What little they have away

Earth stirs again
New bust in the cast

We lost our nude
With breasts big as two pregnant bellies
She lay around on cushions
Too top-heavy to rise
Breasts to cleave hooves   lift sags
   Turning last rites into fertility rites

New bust in the cast
   New Cybele
Yet not so big she can't shake it
   But lie around on cushions
Don't dance it away
The others dance well but bustless

   Nudes to no purpose
We were beginning to think we had burned
The breasts along with the bras
Attendance shrank with our bosoms
   With a new bust in the cast
Watch our box-office swell[24]

---

[23] *Le Sacre du Printemps, The Rite of Spring*, is Igor Stravinsky's ballet depicting primitive tribal life, culminating in the death of the "chosen one," who dances herself to death.

[24] This poem is based on events at the Dramatis Personae Theater on West 14th Street. The "new bust" proved an insufficient audience lure, and the theater finally shifted to an all-male revue.

<150>

ADULT-ERY

Let the French have their adulteries
    Under prismed chandeliers
Let the Latins have their languors
    To storming guitars and heel beats
I have my own way of carrying on
    If my husband ever turns the key
In the lock early
He'll find more grounds for divorce
     Than coffee grounds
A white knight charging into my kitchen
    Mr. Clean on the floor with me
My latest love arrives
By way of the toilet tank
I lift the lid
And there he is in his motor boat
    Standing up   ready
Oh Captain   My Captain
Should my husband lift the lid
    And surprise us
I need only say he's here to freshen
     Thank you Madison Avenue

<151>

RUNAWAY

Runaway,
Pushed away really,
Pushed out of her stepfather's house
    For being a teen reminder
That her mother is older than the new man:
Working in diners for bus fare
Up from Dallas,
She finds a pad in Manhattan
With other runaways,
And a lunch counter job
Where you had to be nice to the manager
    For being under age
When she always thought
You went to bed with somebody
Only to be a star

On the acid with the other kids,
She had a bummer that bedded her into Bellevue,
    Her severed head screaming
To be put back on her body:
More girls than boys in their pad,
    You passed the boys around,
Got passed around with syphilis sauce;
    Took birth control pills,
And syphilis control shots
As if birth a disease along with V. D.

Sunday above the Park boating lake
She wrote home for her doll,
The one she could throw up to the ceiling,
    And catch and hug,
The doll she could talk to
When nobody else would listen,

<152>

A real at-home doll in a pinafore,
   Pink to her pale,
Brown braids instead of her own honey-kink hair,
   Smile just a little sad:
All she asked for was her doll,
But her mother wrote back
She would by no means release the doll
   To a runaway

<153>

MY DAUGHTER'S EYES

Eyes of forest dapplings
A song to your eyes
My folk singing daughter
To your hazel eyes
Why long for my limited blue
When your eyes are the hue
Of whatever you wear
Wherever you are
He who loves your eyes
Loves many yous
Your eyes are blue
They are golden
They are green
Lemon lime in quick starting tears
Root beer drops by the brook
Green in our green ocean
Blue in a Caribbean cove
Golden in desert light
Moist yellow-green of early
Spring leaves   Autumn berries
Summer bloom
Eyes ever seen anew
Are they blue
Are they green
Eyes of hazel
Many hued as your folk songs
Many hued as your moods
Why one hue one finite hue
When you have the infinite in your eyes

<154>

TWAT SHOT
Emilie Glen

TWAT SHOT (1972)

EXITS AND ENTRANCES

Exits and entrances
    Timed wrong on the stage
        And the play is off
    Wrong in life
        And life is off

IN THE NUDE

Nakedness
        Nakedness
Every part he ever played
    A working toward this Eden scene
Performance on performance
    Nudity becomes as every day
        As dogs at the hydrant
Returning to adornment
        He paints his penis gold.

<156>

CRYPT 63

White rose pink,
    Cuddle toy,
Concoction,
    Nature's surprise package,
Imp in a bottle,
    Sunbursts beyond the Louis',
More power than Pompadour,
    Puffed into being down smoke rings,
Public flesh a yummy bit,
    World flesh in a pink cloud around,
Screen flesh real as runway,
    Touchable,
Popcorn, cotton candy, thrill rides,
    Body empire,
So lives   is lived,
    The body
Crypt 63, Case 118572,
    The body found naked in her lone bedroom,
Flesh blue-spotted from the sleeping pills,
    The body wrapped in her own rose blanket,
Strapped to the stretcher,
    Wheeled out the front door
Of the house that flesh built,
    First to the mortuary, then to the morgue,
The morgue in the hall of justice,
    Locked in the storeroom with the brooms and pails,
Mirror to morgue
    All in one night of the body,

News blackprints the papers of the world,
    Flesh universal,
Flesh account,
    Blue-splotched, drugged,
Body in poor condition,
    Dirty fingernails, dirty toenails, brown hair roots,
But never old,
    The young body, pin-up body,

<157>

Strapped to the stretcher,
    Quivering jelly in the carrying out,
The body in the black of the storeroom,
    Tagged for Crypt 63,
Lived as she died,
    The body,
The public body

TOTAL SPREAD

Nude scene
        Through nectarine gauze
Beneath blue and rose gels,
    Ariadne and Theseus fleeing to the Aegean,
Chaste as the new moon,
    The lovers in their dance
None of the genital scratchings at rehearsals
    Nothing of their rehearsal talk
Through the ripplings of a nectarine sea,
    Quit lifting my leg to total spread you prick,
His warnings at certain times
    Not to let her blood drip down on his shoulders,
Twat shot   they dub it,
    Twat shot that gauzes Adriadne and Theseus

<158>

REAL UNREAL

Light it with fireflies
Shine it with mirrors
   The real unreal
   Unreal real
Unreal   your stage life
   My sister screams
To my screaming
   The life you live is unreal
Lighted with blue and amber
   Shubert-pink
      My stage
Real   the breathing of life
   Into my character
Real   the cold sweat of stage fright
   Not sweat of stage work
Lighted amber
   My sister's whiskeyed life
Blood lit   her wrist in drunken slashing
   Life and death   she says

I am my own character
   I write my own script
Stage life   my life
   Its exits   entrances
      Waiting in the wings
There is acting in my sister's suicide attempts
   Life and death in the suicides
      I play under the lights
The unreal real
Real unreal
   Shine it with mirrors
   Light it with fireflies

<159>

CLEFT

Nude
    I stand with flaming sword
Turning every rehearsing moment
       Into undress rehearsal,
Cleft earth to a river of fire,
    Know a man to know a woman know a man,
Missionary angel of the Greek chorus
    I say to the boys backstage,
Burn your middle class values in my river of fire,
    Admit the needs of your nature,
Women not woman and men men ...
Come to me naked in the dark behind the lights,
    Lie with me in the wings,
What are colors without contrast?
    This is the stage,
       The one true stage.
That other stage is only a vestibule,
    Let the principals crowd it,
They're the mortals,
    We're the gods.
Come chorus   come chorus
    Swim my river of fire.
Who are you to call me a pervert?
    You're the pervert knowing only women,
I know men   know women,
      I am all to all,
    Each to every,

I am whole,
 The ones already mine are not enough,
      I need converts   ever more converts,
To prove mine is the way,
It is   isn't it?
    Mine is world Eden,
Don't gather your robes against me,
    Don't make me know my nakedness.

<160>

STRIP

Nudie of our show
Strips at every rehearsal
   Rehearses her bare body
As we rehearse our lines
   Her line or two
She overlooks in posturings
   Before the mirror columns
The gum in her mouth wadding out the words
   Happens to be wearing panties tonight
      That time of month
Bawled out by Madame Director
   For late entrances
She releases rage by ripping off her panties
   Hurling them across the stage
      As if to a crash
We consult psychology books
      Run to Kraft-Ebbing[25]
   To find out if she strips
      To punish her Mother.

---

[25] Kraft-Ebbing's *Psychopathia Sexualis* was a groundbreaking study of sexual perversion and fetishes. It became widely available in English in the 1960s.

<161>

STRAIGHT

Straight
    Walk straight,
  Walk the straight and narrow,
Go straight,
    Tell it straight,
  Are you straight or on the acid?
Are you straight? asked of me
  Means   Do you go for girls?
To tell it straight,
  My male body wants only a male body,
It's the ultimate
  Like the sea,
Like the black night of universe
  Beyond earth's blue atmosphere
The male form,
    Highest fashioning,
  Wound round with my desire,
But just before I go on
    For my sun dance in the nude,
This new girl in the cast,
I guess it was the blue dotted swiss
Clouding about her naked dancer's body
  I took to hugging her
    And twisting her curls,
For her
    In her dotted swiss
I could almost go straight

<162>

CHERISHED

Cherish
   Velvet word of marriage
   Cloak about my shoulders,
   Pillow for my head,
My husband vowed to cherish me,
   We met in scenes class,
   Showcased together,
   Made the rounds,
Were lidded into office jobs
   Waiting for the break
   We're now supposed to have
   As nude partners
Simulating the sex act
Much as I long for stage center
   I wish I could shrink into the flats,
   Wish the lights would blacken,
I don't want to take off my clothes
   And go through the motions,
I don't want him to want me to,
   It garbage grinds our own moments
   He throws me to the lechers
The way Russians of the steppes
   Threw their young from the sleigh
      to wolves,
Putting me in a mirrored brothel,
   That's how he keeps in the theater,
When I tell him of the pinches   the propositions
   He turns up his coat collar against my words,

<163>

It's his role he guards fiercely,
    The white-gold spotlight he holds in his arms,
I would rather have him veil my face.
    Hide me away from the world on some
        far mountain top
Dream I keep dreaming,
      He tears down the stage curtain
      And covers me,
      Beats back the crowd
    Bearing me off to a bed of flower petals
      Where I am his alone

SCRIPT IN HAND

    Rain in my face
    Wind through my hair
Snow crunching to a path under my feet
The surfing in of starfish
    All of that and a wave to ride
To have a script in my hand
    Actually Rainbow spray
      But it has a sure heft
    Solid yet dream textured
A new role to know
      Your stage room
      Your stage being
    Too white new to be put away
Script in the beginning
      A winged white horse
    Sun galloping to great stage

<164>

GLENDA'S ARK (1970)

DIRTY DOG

Dirty dogs are we?
When we're that dirty
We call one another dirty people,
You live in your dirt and I'll live mine,

Fight your wars like ants,
We'll fight dog to dog
And bite you only in rabies,
You have your plastic this,
Your nylon that,
You've made me people enough
To jump for a bone of nylon,
So don't mess in my life,
Stop saying not even fit for a dog,
Just give me my nylon bone
And I won't bark what I think of you

GONE

Little cat lost to us
Be somewhere
Oh be somewhere
Our window sill frames no fur portrait
Furniture no longer for leaping
Guitar picks and walnut shells
No longer pawed to floor timpani
House still as the turning globe

Little cat
Sun through the rooms
No longer shapes you
Be somewhere
Oh be somewhere
Corners back to being only corners
Your green striped bowl is by the stove
Your catnip mouse under the sofa

<166>

You are not velveting over to us
   Waking us with a nose lick
  Snapping your ears
Where is your pink yawn
  Be somewhere
    Little cat
Oh be somewhere

SPOTSY

I'm a giraffe
  I nibble leaves
My neck stretches tall
  I'm way up here
My legs up me
   Call me camelopard
    If you like
I share that name
   With a constellation
    Hard as I kick
I'd rather run
    Rather hide
  Let my orange spots
   My sun extrusions
Dapple me into leaf shade
  I'm a giraffe
And the lions hunt me
Ready to tear my flesh
When I only nibble leaves

<167>

PET PILOSA

Catta Pilosa
    My caterpillar's Latin name
I walk him out on a leash
    Never have to curb him
        He does it dainty
Lemony fur
    With white guard hairs
        Like a mink of special breed

Catta Pilosa
        Deeper piled than my rug
I have him treated
    So he won't roll up in a cocoon
Come out a butterfly
    And fly away from me

REVENGE OF THE BEASTS

Revenge of the beasts
    My piano tuner tells me
Through the vibrations of his tuning fork,
    One day it will come,
        The revenge of the beasts,
A calf is easily bound and slaughtered
        My little girl sings,
    Easily bound and slaughtered
        Never knowing the reason why

Revenge of the beasts,
    He repeats it often as the notes
        He brings to perfect tune,
Revenge of the beasts,
    Deer topaz-eyed in the car lights,
The giraffe nibbling mimosa leaves,

<168>

The seals of Northern seas,
Revenge of the beasts,
    The beaver gnawing off his feet
To be free of the agony trap,
    Rabbits driven into a clearing,
And beaten in a bunny bash,
        Fun   fun,
Seals skinned alive in the rush
    To put furs on the rack,
Open heart of a sea lion
    Pumping blood into a dying body,
Gentle horses turned bucking bronco
    By a strap that tortures the intestines,

The young starving to death
    Without their Mothers,

For every zoo delight
    A thousand animals died in anguished passage,
Revenge of the beasts,
    Maimed by don't-care hunters,
Animals vivisected,
    Given dread diseases,
Geese in painful fattening of their livers
    For *pâté de fois gras*,
Cattle hung to bleed to death,
    Live and don't let live,
The whale   great sea cow,
    See how fiercely the creature thrashes
        Stuck with harpoons.
Hook fish   leave them to gasp for breath
        As we would gasp in their sea,
Be slap-happy with pesticides   leaking oil
    That takes away the flight of birds

The globe a huge slaughter-house   pain house
    With depressed rim round it to collect the blood

<169>

Man shall have dominion,
      Cruel dominion
Because man says God says he has dominion,
      Jealous we have no fur   no feathers,
            Have no wild,
We pour cement   ever pour cement,

Revenge of the beasts,
      It's starting,
The butcher whose knife is turned in
            On his own belly
   By a calf twisting in pain.

The desperate deer discharges the hunter's gun
            Into his gut.
Lurching after forest creatures
   Hunters keep on killing hunters.
May they die slow,
Slow as the life they maim,
Bring it   piano tuner,
      Bring it with every quiver of your tuning fork,
            Revenge
                  Revenge of the beasts

LUCY VON HEIMENSCHNEIDER

Lucy
      Our house guest
Lucy Von Heimenschneider
            Properly introduced
She is supposed to be here
            Briefly
   Which is too long
She knocks over our knick-knacks
   Breaks glasses
      Tracks dirt
   Worse   she wets

<170>

Shits short of the cat-box
The couple who dropped off Lucy
        Must have fled to the Argentine
Lucy Von Heimenschneider
            Appears to be our kitten
At sight of our sofa down to the wood
    Our arms and legs bleeding from her claws
We dial an adoption agency
        Hang up
      Hung up
            On Lucy
The kitten who came to tuna

FLIC UNDER THE SUN

Tiny item
        In the cellar of the news,
It mouse-creeps into my heart,
        Up in the living-room of large
I read about deaths
        By earthquake   plane crash   shell-fire
Thousands here   thousands there
Not much more than a math lesson

Tiny down,
        The penguin Flic,
He touches me,
        Stolen from a zoo in Rome,
Taken from his cool pool,
        If he is not found soon
He will die of the heat
        In his little dress-suit,
His flippers will flap away his life,
        Flic from the Antarctic
Dying in the Rome sun
        Not knowing why,
It touches me,
        It touches me

<171>

EMPTY

Hearts in hock
Noses in shit
They're trying to put through a bill
Banning dogs from apartment buildings
But my apartment is empty
Even if I have a house in the mountains
A house by the sea
My rooms will be empty
I will never be calling
Be calling a dog to me
For his leap   his lick
Brown eyes all mine

My dog   my dachshund
On his inadequate little legs
I was eleven when I last called to him
To anyone
Velvet   I named him
For he was brown velvet
I called across the street
To my friend Elbert
And my friend Velvet
Hearing it as his name
Came running on his groundling legs
Running in all trust
To his death under a car

Oh he didn't die right away
Blood and pain in my arms
And one last look   all mine
If it hadn't happened so fast
I would have thrown myself in front of the car
For Velvet
That is why my rooms are empty
Why I never call

<172>

TIPSIE

Oriental Princess
                We call her
Oriental Princess of the Quarter Moon
    White kitten
                    Not as long as her name
White with a black quarter moon on her brow
    Moon for short
Or Tipsie for the black tip of her tail
    We try to be one with her
But she is a very private person
    Her treasure   a kitten-sized skip rope
                  She secures between
                      Her somewhat teeth
Hides it from us
    Whenever she stops skipping
In the shower stall   back of the stereo
                  Behind the radiator
Now we don't know where
    We can afford our princess privacy
        Princess of the Quarter Moon

<173>

ROAST SWAN (1984)

OF A FEATHER

MOURNING MORNING

Mourning dove
   on the fire escape across
Mourning dove nesting
   where the blinds are never lifted
Feathers muted pink   muted blue
dark peacock spots
Mourning dove
   should be morning dove
   nesting morning
sits through thunder   lightning
   gale winds
my heart hurts
   over the precarious nesting
If we tossed her food
   we would scare her away
Through binoculars we see the babies born
see the cinder eye of one downy
   shining jewel in the sun
Night hides the nest
   no medicaid   no welfare
for the mourning dove

PIGEON COLONNADE

Times Square pigeons
   performers all
especially ones ledging
   on the Doric colonnade
of the the old Keith Palace
Actors reincarnate
   who made the rounds below
   trying for the Broadway stage

<176>

ON WALL STREET

Oven bird on Wall Street
    hesitation waltz about the bush
oven bird on Wall Street
      looking into his holdings
      in Trinity graveyard
      stocking up before winging South
      for the winter
Wall Street graveyard at one end
    river at the other
and an ovenbird
      bringing the lunch hour crowd
          back to basics

DRAGONS DO

Dragons do the dishes
The flamenco storming manager
    of the café where I play the piano
dragons his passion   the fiercest
    must have claws   no belly crawlers
Dragons do the dishes
as I try to shake the wheezing piano to life
    Dragons do the dishes
    in the café depths
      beyond the ruby candle glow
do the dishes
    but they eat the tables   the chairs
      the flamenco guitar
        in its coffin case
eat the café while doing the dishes

<177>

TRULY

I saw the wind today
   Yes I did   I saw it
Truth child
You know you can't see the wind
Only where it's going   where it's been
What it touches
Yes I did
   I saw the wind
   Saw it through field-glasses
Truth truth
It's wiggly-smooth like vanilla icing
Only it isn't white or gray or any color
   It's not glass like heat waves
I saw the wind truly I did
   A billion bird feet across the bay
Wiggling away the snowy egrets
     by the reeds
   Making off with the glossy ibises
   Wadding up my lenses
I saw the wind
Saw the wind today

<178>

ROAST SWAN

What do you drink
     with roast swan?
  What wines while you cut meat
  from the bones
  of the tall white glider of waters?
White wine? red?
  one of the rosés
for feathers roseate with sunset?
    Do you dine to the wine tones
    of *Swan Lake?*
What do you drink with roast swan?
    Why not roast the wine
    and let the swan fly free?

<179>

IN B-FLAT MINOR

MY GRAND

Grand Duchess
>Grandmother
>Grand daughter

Grand Lama
>Grand Slam

Grand should be reserved
>for my grand piano
>Grew up with my grand

My grand moved miles
>Is ailing from river damp

Sounding board cracked
>Rending of the veil
>The temple veil

Plague of moths at the felts
>In the dust of a haunted house

Its mahogany like crackleware
>Scratches   gashes
>Bleeding white

Not enough money to put it in drydock
>For a launching down the waves

My piano   my grand
Perhaps someone will buy
Pay the thousands for reconditioning
>And it will live high above the Park

Beneath a fire glinting chandelier

<180>

No one buys
    I've seen scrapped grands
Strings crazing   keyboard upended
    dogs wetting
Sounding board axed for kindling wood
I play the Chopin Prelude
    I did at a recital when I was six
    Storm a Polonaise
Before calling the Bureau of Encumbrances

<181>

GROTESQUES

IN REPLY

In reply
    Surface Transit
Reply to your
    Surface Transit and
Letter
    Operating Company
Postmarked
   November 15th
Our Mr. Techener
Has handled your complaint
      Bus driver
With dispatch
      Badge number 1058
Was duly beheaded
   At 5:02
Tuesday November 17th
As soon as the blood dries
   And the axle grease is removed
     From the forearms
You may draw and quarter the body
   In our offices 79-59
    Matson Boulevard
Bring your own utensils
    We must inform you
   That we stand on our rights
    To retain the head

<182>

DOUGHNUTS HOLES

Off to school with his invisible dog
my little son walks him to a
      tensioned leash
  passersby bend down to pet
Watch out   he bites
Know what he eats?
   Evaporated water
      and doughnut holes
He enters the school invisible
with his invisible dog

TIME CLOCK

He tore out the time clock
   where we punch in   punch out
   punch in   in   out
Ripped it from the wall
   Bells bonging   wires pinging
   to a jangle
Ripped himself out of the business day.
   In his honor
I'm not wearing my wristwatch tomorrow
   I open the window almost wide enough
      to blow my papers out the window
   in tickertape parade

<183>

DIRTY

Dirty children
   screaming over the removal of dirt
Jungian perhaps
   in racial feel of earth
not wanting to be too close to godliness
Fastidious me
   was I ever like that
supposed to have said
    My thumbs don't need washing
      they hang in
My little son,
   could he have penis fright
   over the removal of any part of him?

Occupationally sound
He can be a gardener   Con Ed digger
   be a garage mechanic spread tar
be on the commercial that calls for a dirt
   looking for something to soil

<184>

PLANT HELL

My plants
   the hanging ones
   the window box blooms
I bought them for their quietude
Lately they're quaking me
   especially the petunias
ever since I learned they can
  read my thoughts
can pout if I seem to give other flowers
   more attention
their sensitivity has been duly tested
psycho-galvanic analyzers
   mitogenetic rays
   integratons   polygraphs
    magnetic fields
audio-oscillator electrodes
Plants shudder at cruel intent
whether to rip off a leaf or cut a stem
I lock myself away from them
until I learn I can be miles away
   and they will know my state of mind
My tomato vines my chives
   carrots   radishes
such screams at uprooting they force me
   to become
   a meat-atarian

What if I became tempted to enter
   into a plant
   for a while   a forever while
My hostility is so obvious that my plants
   are now dying in their hanging baskets
the petunias dead in their window boxes
   I am replacing them with plastic roses

<185>

PUTRESCENCE

Dead
   Murdered
      by me
   your lover
Not enough   nowhere near enough
anymore than the rapids
    ending in the falls
      bomb in the burst
What was you   lies putrescing
      in that trunk
    your stink in my nostrils
      in the closet floorboards
you who tried to leave me
    running away towards

Only I can take your gagging stench
    Your brown liquid seeps
    into the floorboards
The couple below complain   disinfect
    think a dead squirrel must be
      rotting in the wall
You are no longer a name   a face
    a running up the stairs to me
    in floats of chiffon
      about your jeans
Putrescent   my love

<186>

CREDIT

Credit cards
    only their credit cards
twenty years later
    survived the crash
All else rotted into jungle moss
    along with their Piper Cub
only their credit cards survived
    oh, and their bones

I DIED IN THE NIGHT

Dying in the night
    this I could take
as I took the seasons
not that it was quite my season
    in the fullness of forty
but to be a body found
    after eleven days
    acquaintances blabbering
press announcing
    BODY BADLY DECOMPOSED
    discovered by its stink
when I was always so free of BO
In the obits I was cited
    for my ornithological findings
    even if no bird was named after me
The Linnaean Society in needless guilt
    planted *In Memoriam* a black cherry
to attract birds I may train
    to peck at their eyes
    for I plan to haunt horribly
Ghosts are the ones who died dissatisfied
    I'm planning to haunt everyone
    who knows it took eleven days
    to find me by my stink

<187>

CATO'S MIDNIGHT

DEAF

Stone deaf
  My mother
    So the grownups say
How deaf is a stone
    Do stones close her ears to my voice
I run out into the fields
      of our Vermont farm
    Gather stones from before speech
Six boulders warmed by the summer sun
    Wondering   can they hear
      Through cracks and crevices
crawl into the cool of a cave
      stone womb of silence
I communicate with my deaf Mother
    like stone-age people
      in signs and gestures
        and wordless sounds
Grow up to be a geologist
with stone-age discoveries
Follow rock faults across country
    still wondering
      How deaf is a stone

<188>

TO LET

FURNISHED ROOM TO LET
    The sign hangs for him,
Big man   his arms reach wall to wall,
    A washbasin by the airshaft window,
        bathroom on the floor below:
Graying hair grand as an astrakhan hat,
    features for a Dutch painting;
Still he is a waif, an odd-job man,
The waif   the old waif,
    brings to his furnished room,
        a young waif
a hitch-hiking girl
    shaking with chills,
    burning with fever,
Heats broth for her on his one burner;
    spoons out cherry-flavored cough medicine
        to ease her bronchial spasms;
Brings her chicken breasts and petit fours
    His own meal less gourmet.
Seeks to cool her fever
    reading to her from the *Upanishads,*
        Her cough choking off his words:
Books he will have, second-hand but books;
    If he could get in on some training program
        he'd do better by her, find an apartment

His family escaped the Polish pogroms
    to give him the chance
        he somehow missed:
nobody believes a poor Jew possible.

    His father dealt in remnants
from one of those pushcarts
    where your head and torso stick up
through the middle like a man sawed in half:

<189>

His father a whole man only
    at the dinner table   such as it was,
and at his cello

When her fever burns low,
when her cough almost leaves her,
   he comes back from painting
      someone's apartment
to find her gone like a butterfly
   out over the sea
He sits down to his soup, wondering,
   Is she ill somewhere,
   ill and alone?

<190>

PINCHES THE PEACHES

Pinches the peaches.
   Pings the crystal.
      Peers under linings,
Scrutinizes the selvage,
   Examines package labels
Down to pounds ounces glutamates,
   Third degrees salespersons,
But in the choosing of a second mate
   She pins the tail on the donkey

<191>

CATO'S MIDNIGHT

Little Cato sitting
   on the midnight doorstep
     of café street
waiting for his mother to leave
   whatever bar
waiting to see her up the stairs
    If his name weren't Cato
    If his glasses weren't quite so owl
I wouldn't care to bursting
   There he sits into midnight
   on the doorstep of their walk-up
waiting for his mother
   his reeling-lurching lid-heavy
     mother
   who may be with one of his many uncles
There   he will always sit
   whatever desk may be his
   whatever steering wheel
with whatever tools   in whatever art
   whatever night room
   he tries to take his rest
he will be waiting to help her
   up the midnight stairs

<192>

CUT HER WRISTS

Mama is all bloody at my
    birthday party,
      Everyone says it's nice to be six,
Mama is in the bedroom,
    Blood coming through
        the bandages on her wrists,
I have balloons to blow up,
    My face getting
      red enough to pop blood,
Aunt Ellen is in with Mama
    When she's supposed
    to be seeing to my birthday

Doorbell,
    They're coming they're coming
      Coming with presents
I'm not supposed to open them
    until after we cut
      the birthday cake,
But Mama isn't out here to say No,
    I can do just as I please

Aunt Ellen on the phone,
    saying Mama
    cut her wrists with a razor
On account of Daddy not being here,
    not giving her any money,

She cut her wrists
    to let all the blood out
    so she'd be dead as my goldfish
      its body bent funny

<193>

My Aunt got the blood
   in the bathroom
   almost wiped up
     when the first bell rang,
Peter's Daddy wanting to know
   where is Mama,
     and I said sleeping.
I wish her blood would stop bleeding
   and she'd come to my party
     and help me cut the cake.
She makes magic of everything
   A party without Mama
   is like a party
     without balloons

Aunt Ellen won't let me go to Mama,
   Wish I could unwrap her
   all laughing and well,
Forgive me baby Mama kept saying,
   Some day you'll understand,
She forgets this is my sixth birthday
   and I know a lot,
How Daddy has to do with this,
   and I'm not enough
   to make it up to her,

I don't want my party anymore,
   I don't want to be six,
Don't want to grow up and be Mama.
   I'm going into the bathroom
and I'm going to make a blood faucet
     of my wrists,
   and be a funny bent fish

<194>

PEAR TREE

Outlived them
outlived the seven
    I wrote them into my will
        when I lay dying
The pear tree outside
    my apartment window
    stared into it until I became
    the perfect pear of health
stared so root nourished deep
I outlived them
outlived the seven
beat my grieving chest
    in Tarzan outcry
    Rewriting my will
I can't conjure seven
nor six nor five nor four
    only two
but I'll outlive
I the partridge in the pear tree

<195>

DADDY'S OLD SPICE

Mama Mama look
    Daddy's Old Spice
    he's too dead to need it anymore
The little boy runs out of the closet
    that hides big black bears in the dark
More fun than a pillow fight
    shaking the powder about
spices his toys with white drifts
whitens his hair with the spicy snow
makes him sneeze and sneeze
every room smelling like Daddy
    after shave

DON'T

Lady
      Lady   Lady
          stop catering
Why do you suppose I chose the sea
    wish you never learned to knit
It's plain food I want
    spare me your sauces   your stir-fries
refrain from quilting my coffin
    Lady   if I'm ever a flower garden
please don't cultivate me

<196>

WHY DOES HE HATE MIRO

Father from the gypsy caves above Triana
Mother from the coffee hills of Puerto Rico
   the five-year-old looks up at me
   with eyes too dark for pupils
to bloom Spanish pride
I point to a painting by Miro
   Dark deep he looks at the splashing gold
My father hates that
Hates Miro   Why
Why does he hate Miro
My father hates everything beautiful
Why   why everything beautiful
Because he works so hard

I ASSASSINATE

Asass   assass   assassinate
   assassination fantasies
   my well water of wine
The Castro fantasy
   worth setting to music
I lace soot-beard's plantains
   with ground glass
   which will perforate his intestines

Whenever I am about to assassinate
   an African usurper
     someone does it for me
Don't suppose I'll have a chance
   at Khomeini

As the smiling assassin
I smile in to a car window
before shooting the death ray
   concealed in my contact lenses
Nasser I drowned in an oil drum

<197>

Hitler
    I would have posed
    as a missile salesman
Mussolini
    I'd have built a faulty balcony

Assass assass
    I'll never go to a shrink
for without my fantasies
    I'm a heap of rags
Still my fantasies
    don't quite satisfy
    I must assassinate
      someone for real
if I can find anyone worthy
    of my assassination

<198>

ENOUGH

Inappropriate
    octopus words
    swelling with poison ink
    to burst my face blue
Inappropriate
    my husband's word
    at my lapses from decorum
    and they are as many
        as desert cacti
Inappropriate
    jeans with high heels
Inappropriate
    to collect like greeting cards
    my teen-age son has appropriated
        the word to ice me over
I'm so inappropriate
    there's nothing left for me
        but to go abscam

<199>

D-A-V-I-D

Slivered almonds burning
    I teach a neighbor boy
    to write his name
burning in burned butter sauce
    David   David
    the boy with the slingshot
    David the King
    David coveting Bathsheba
D — a straight line holding the new moon
A — an upside down V with a bar across
    Almonds burning
N ext the V right side up
I — straight
Again the D straight line
    half circle
Your name begins with D
    ends with D
David   David
that's it
    you have written your name
for all the checks
    the legal documents
    duplicates   triplicates
Sign here and here and here and here
David known   David unknown
David   D-A-V-I-D
    slivered almonds burned black

<200>

SEED PEARLS

Down the aisle in my wedding gown
      ivory sewn with seed pearls
My family couldn't afford
      so much as a strip of its lace
         unless recycled

Down the aisle in my recycled gown
I'll recycle mine back to the shop
         where I bought it
      when all this is over
Rather honest of me to march
        toward the reverend
      in a recycled gown
since you see
      when it comes to virginity
      I too am recycled

<201>

GIANT

Chased by a
Yes by a
giant
Sue   I must
chased in every nightmare
by a
chased by a giant coke bottle
about to explode in my face
nightmare dumped on me
ever since a supermarket coke bottle
exploded in my hand

Awarded a modest sum
considering
two thousand dollars
for shock
psychiatrist bills
for wasting sleepless
away
denied the pleasures
of the bubblies
of shopping
in wide-aisled supermarkets
Forever being chased
across deserts
over mountains
through bogs
down thruways
by a giant coke bottle
about to explode

<202>

LORD OF THE LAKE

LIQUID LILAC

Theater streets ago
    Papa took me to a play
I am the Wanderer
    the man kept saying
    beneath a sky of liquid lilac
making the lilacs by our kitchen window
    in to a wandering forever
Didn't know from where to where for what
    no sky since as lilac lighted

Today I wander
    not knowing as Galahad knew
when he went searching for the Holy Grail
    blood red upon the mountains
    blood red across the seas
Jason definitely after the Golden Fleece

My wandering may be backwards
    after a broken doll
    leaflights in my night room
A goodnight never said
    award I didn't win
or just the lilac sky
    of the Wanderer

<203>

WILLARD

Willard
    there was a boy named Willard
Willard
    I speak your name after five years,
        leap you alive,
    my brother alive,
Lord of the lake for the poise, the plunge
    powered strokes to the far out.
You stand in ropes of light,
    blond hair sun-streaked,
        shoulders jeweled by lake water,
sixteen to my water-scared nine,
strongest swimmer of the shore

Willard
    I speak you alive
        after years of no remembering,
alive to drown in the stone-green lake
    blacked by storm,
no chance in your hunting boots,
    bound by slimed reeds.
        through weeks of dragging the bottom,
Held my breath in the night
    to see if drowning is as easy as they say

Willard
    You would be middle-aged by now
        hair thinning   body thickened.
You would be settled off some place,
    an engineer in Venezuela
        or a lawyer in Oregon.

<204>

I wouldn't like your wife much
    nor reunions at the shore,
You would be teaching
    your own children to swim

Willard
    There was a boy named Willard
You taught me to trust the waters,
    hands in   come-on,
You can do it   You can swim,
    Even the black seal ring
        found on your finger
        lasts in my jewel box,
    helmeted head of a warrior.
You never grew up to be maimed in a war
    but the coffin had to be closed,
I saw it from the window
    being carried down the steep steps,

Willard
    Drowned these many years
        in the stone-green lake
           of no remembering
You struggle up through the binding reeds,
        the muddy bottom,
    struggle up to breathing,
stand for the speaking of your name,
    shoulders jeweled by lake water,
strongest swimmer of the shore

SOUR ANGELS

Brownstone gravestones
   in the red of old fires,
sour little angel heads
   exfoliate in the churchyard
beside the street of air-brakes
     and diesels;
    I walk among them in winter rain,
     earth sponge-rubber
     grass tired green,
waiting to go on in a fairy-tale
   older than these stones
   of the seventeen hundreds
The graves are ancient,
   but those who lie here,
     they are young,
the Abigails   Elizas   Charitys
   Calebs   Joshuas   Ezras,
Rufus who departed this world
   In the twenty-third year of his days,
   Two years I bore affliction sore,
   Physicians were in vain,
   The Lord alone He heard my moan,
   And saved me from my pain
The young died mostly in the winter
   For Elizabeth it was summer
The sixteenth summer of her days,
   Fields for running,
   waters for swimming
The debt is Paid,
The grave you see,
Prepare for death and follow me,

<206>

Katherine 7   Christopher 5   Amy 12
Seventeen the third day of May,
        trees first-leafing,
    all around me the young,
        the long ago young
I had always run past
    on my way to the stage,
I run now,
    hands numb with cold,
        feet wet with rained earth
to play an old-young tale,
    for the children are coming
already they are coming.

WOULD I

One see
    granted if I were blind
would I choose
    a night of stars
    Moses' tablets of stone
    the lost Atlantis
    eagle's nest
        a daisy?
One see
    your face

<207>

TENTACLED

Blue eyed squid
Blue eyed me
    resent squid blinking blues
squid's blue eyes stare me back
        into the sea
    out of which I crawled
tentacled   blue eyed tentacled
suppose I swim tentacled too
fast fierce and blue

CRAVINGS

Tonight we speak our cravings,
    the ones we keep in rose quartz,
I reach for a whiff of horse droppings,
    pluck lilac florets one by one
    to suck the nectar

My cravings grey down
    before the cravings told round me:
"I like to chew on knotted string,
    smell my dog's paws."

"I eat newspapers at the edges
    where there is no print,
not yesterday's paper,
    it has to be today's."

"I wrap old socks about my throat,
boil buttons."

"I knock on firehouse doors,
    and run,
snap clay pipes."

<208>

"I wad carbon paper,
   get blue with it
      and wash my hands."

"I taste chalk,
   enjoy fish scales more than fish meat."

"Don't knock it.
   I fingerpaint with toothpaste,
      it has a crushed leaf smell.

"This I swore I'd never admit
   much as I try to resist
I like to   like to
   No   I can't say it."

"I squeeze clams.
   pop tar bubbles,
heel the soft tar into craters."

"Now I'm not proud of this,
   I turn pages just to crack
      the book bindings."

"I relish buttered pussy willows."

For all their sparkle water
   I'll keep on smelling
      horse droppings
    sucking lilacs.

<209>

GOLDEN

Eyes of the deer
      golden fire in the night
deer tender as young birch trees
      harming no one
the dark hills red sunned hills
      leap with deer
Welcome signs in stores and restaurants
      of the hill town
Could it be welcome in winter wither
for the deer with the golden eyes

WELCOME DEER HUNTERS
real estate operators advertise
temporary tracts of land for the hunters
      driving the highway
with its deer crossing signs
      seeming to protect
   we see hunters in red caps   blood caps
lusting to kill   maim   when the deer
   come down to drink at evening
doing the deer a favor say the hunters
they would starve

Don't kill   feed them through the winter
      the hills are beating
      with the hearts of terrored deer
Cars pass us with dead deer tied to the roof
One car passes close
      two limp deer strapped down
      their golden eyes open

<210>

In the name of the golden fire
if we were hunters we would want to aim
at the hunters   aiming at deer
        who never harmed anyone
Behind our foresting lids at night
        when we return from the hills
golden eyes of dead deer

<211>

WITH WHAT CIRCUS

WRIGGLES BETWEEN

Poetry meets a four-year-old
We sit in a Tuesday circle
   reading our poetry to one another
A poem herself
  she wriggles between
  two poets on the sofa
listens   her eyes solemn blues
   announces she has a poem
     begins spider spinning
Crackers crackers
flying to crumbs
mice and cheese and crackers
mice on tiny feet crackers crackers
spider thread spins slow
crackers her smile halos
   crackers you eat
     you eat crackers
  mice   mice you don't
    you don't eat mice
She climbs down off the sofa
   to depart in her space machine
   leaving us to ponder creation

<212>

OPEN READING

Poets in open readings
    shuffle their papers
    shuffle their papers
shuffles that would never win at cards
shuffles that distinguish us from theater
    scrap papers   legal size
    triptychs   notebooks
    ledgers fit for Uriah Heep[26]
mostly hand written
    the particular poem they want
    buried as in leaves for a bonfire
    or a bonfire for leaves

Poets' papers a band of urchins
    in need of baths
might better write on oysters
    and dive for the pearls
Papers   papers
    a rustling of poets' wings
    bringing the word

---

[26] Uriah Heep. A villainous clerk in Charles Dickens' *David Copperfield*.

<213>

WITH WHAT CIRCUS

What do you do
   What
     what

I'm a clown

Oh with what circus

Cosmos and Company

Do you paint your face
and put on big feet

No I paint my interior
and put on a big head.

What do you do   really

Nothing really
   only ideally

Really   ideally
   what

I stretch my giraffe neck
   and nibble mimosa leaves
     by moonlight

You're very circus minded

Yes I mind the animals
   in my computer ringed circus

I juggle golden apples
   Saw myself in half

<214>

A clown *and* a magician then

    Then and now
    Now and then
I cut my wrists
    and birds fly out
If I start pulling ribbons
    out of my sleeves
    you'll have the seven rings of Saturn
My hair is a star fall

What sign were you born under

All of them by way of marzipan

Marzipan is not a sign

    It is for me
I make flower bombs
    blow them up to bursting petals

Where can I catch your act

Anywhere   everywhere
        Sky up

And what do you do
when you're not clowning

    I die
Blow up like a big black balloon
        and burst with it.

<215>

SKY LADDER

Sounds of a city summer night
windows open to everyone's sky ladder
   chicken-yard pecks of typewriters
   guitar in learning strums
scales voice   piano
The air must tray with all this
     humid reach
   only the painter's brush is silent

<216>

STREET MERCURY

Mercury
  this messenger
Mercury without wings
neither swift across violet mountains
nor swift down city streets
he pushes his reluctant feet along
up curb down curb
elevators up up down
his eyes blear at traffic
he lives meatless
 in the one furnished room
 allotted him on a messenger's pay
Messenger
 wingless Mercury
 from the mountains of Greece
 from grey-eyed Athene's gaze

he is growing the great American play
  in his head
 all things are possible
 for he is Mercury
stops by a building pauses in a lobby
 to take notes
If it isn't sleet stinging
 nor chill raining
 even if it is
he gives himself a Park break
 by the fountain
writing with purple fingers fat with cold
 on the pencil stub
a snowman sometimes

Down the hall and to the right
down and to the left
falls asleep over the typewriter
 his characters saying saying
saying what

<217>

ROUNDS

Eleven callbacks
Come seven   come eleven
can't just can't
be left off on an anonymous street
not me with the fire of Bernhardt
    tears of Duse
Making the rounds
    brings fever to my night pillow
Auditions   shut my mouth with sand
only to know in the loss of my love
    nothing hurts like the heart

<218>

MATTER OF TASTE

Hazardous
   for you to write a poem
on the back of an old menu
   expecting a critique
How can I comment on worlds
   beyond worlds
when peeking at the menu
   I taste duck with orange glaze
   trout in sauce almandine
   baked alaska   crêpes suzette
How can you lift me to your poetry
   by way of Hawaiian steak
   London broil
   chicken à la Kiev
Friend
   I fear the poetry is all in the menu

<219>

HOW IS IT WITH INFINITY

HALLOWED BE THY

Our Great Machine which art in outer space
Hallowed be Thy Name
    Thy computer come
    Thy digits be done
on this planet as on telestar
Give us this day our daily oil
Forgive us our nuclear errors
    as we forgive the blown reactors of others
Lead us not into too great a grab
and deliver us from energy crises
for Thine is the kingdom
    the power and the glory
        forever
                AMACHINE

<220>

OFFICIAL

First official
        day of Spring
    the computers are blooming
The computers are blooming
    at IBM,
        blooming among flowers under glass,
            full summered under glass
cineraria in pink and purple sunburst,
        a Caribbean of orchids,
    Birds of Paradise
        planted in the imported soil
    along with computer parts
        more delicate than the blooms,
more Spring
    this first official day

Magnetic doughnuts
    glitter minutely
in bowls centering prickle plants,
    "And the desert shall bloom like a rose,"
IBM writes *Mene, Mene, Tekel, Upharsin,*
    Tiny doughnut-shaped cones
store masses of information
        in very little space,
    bright as the first robin
on the first official day,
    abstract art among the orchids,
        gold traceries in metal collage,

<221>

Circuit modules the glass writes,
    cacti more rigid
        than the chip transistors,
tiny white ceramics
        bending on wire stems
    as if to the breeze,
over in the rock garden
    oh the warp and the woof
        in pastel greens and orange,
Web of memory cores says the window
    Magnetic-memories
of lily-of-the-valley by the porch
    Skunk cabbage just opening
        down by the creek,
Jack-in-the-pulpit and violets
        in the deeper grass

Over all is the great computer
    all lights and levers,
sly juke box with cinematic reels,
    viewed by passersby
        as they would view the body,
our new brain laid out before us
    among the plantings
    to be programmed
        with memories of Spring

<222>

COMPUTERIZED

Under the buttonwood tree
they would gather
      under the buttonwood tree
    the Wall Street merchants of 1792
The buttonwood tree fell
    to the Stock Exchange

On the way to my broker
I'd like to pause beneath the buttonwood
    talk with the merchants
leaf shadows instead of the running lights
    of the big board
voices minding with leaves
    in harbor breezes
more wisdom don't you think
    under the buttonwood tree

<223>

HOW IS IT WITH INFINITY

Infinity experts
I've read to tatters.
How space is time is space,
space-time continuum:
How the universe is probably expanding,
galaxies moving away from us
in red shift:
How stars die,
not with a whimper but with a bang
I know that not one particle is ever lost,
only transmuted:
That light rays are bent
and atoms dance infinity
But when I think infinity
I slip back to child,
remembering the eight candles
on my birthday cake
and how in blowing them out
I was afraid somebody bigger
could blow out the world

In my night room
I would hear the Minister's words
as if corning out of great organ pipes,
World without end Amen,
World without end   without end
without end,
and I would kneel at the window
looking up past poplars
to stars beyond stars beyond stars,

There must be an end to them
like the last daisy
in a field you run,

<224>

but there is always another field,
and another field and another field,
    Daisies   daisies and daisies
        farther than the eye can run
    Day is no time to figure out infinity,
you have to close your eyes
        to the dark within the dark,
World without end   without end
        without end:
    How can the world go on and on forever?
There has to be a rim
    and something beyond the rim
        and beyond the rim

But something has to be out there
        to put the last rim in.
How can it be a world
        unless you can come to the edge,
even the ocean a far shore you can't see,
        And if the world started somewhere,
doesn't it have to end somewhere?
    Is it forever night and windless,
        dark and windless and waveless,
nothing and nothing and nothing?
    Even nothing must be
        contained in something,
star stepping-stones
        in the night of forever:

  What is forever?
    A thing? Then it ends,
World without end
    Amen   has to exist in something,
and if it never started and never ends,
    I fall asleep somewhere beyond
        and beyond and beyond,
    fall asleep over infinity,
        How can it be?

<225>

TOUGH

Tough turkey
 tough turkey on Thanksgiving Day
  Pilgrims partaking
Tough turkey
 under the knife
 stringy white meat woody dark meat
  rubber skin
Tough turkey
 our hostages still in Iran
  bandaged blind
corn yellow ribbons
 on the trunks of trees
oil drying
 drought across the land
ravaged earth killing streams

interest rates climbing
 prices shredding purses
strikes layoffs welfare cheats
  crime blooding our streets
  the paving stones cry out
Tough turkey by harvest light
Tough turkey on Thanksgiving day
  Pilgrims arriving
   on rocks not theirs
Tough tough turkey

<226>

CRACK OF DOOM

Crack crack crack crack
   crack crack crack of doom
Terrible as an army with banners
   the nuclear plant
   of Three Mile Island
      on its way to meltdown
more terrible than an army
      with banners
   atomic energy for peace
Harrisburg in a crouch
   beneath the cooling towers
   reflected red
      in the Susquehanna sunset

Crack crack   crack crack crack
TV voices shouting
   around the radioactive bubble
   stay   evacuate   stay   evacuate
Nuclear engineers flown in
      from around the world
called nuke town
   in easy familiarity
   Officials of the power company
smiling over the bubble
   nicely shrinking
cars kill millions   coal miners die
   but we keep on driving
most accidents take place in the home

<227>

Crack crack crack crack   doom crack
reversing the desert shall bloom
     like a rose
cooling towers shaped like the jars
of a gargantuan Ali Baba
     and the Forty Thieves
     fallout to the grass cows munch
Iodine 131 in their milk
milk and honey become milk
     and thyroid cancer
fissioning uranium producing
     such radioactive isotopes
     as strontium   krypton   xenon   cesium
     rubidium   cobalt
crack crack crack crack
doom crack

<228>

WHERE NOW

Andromeda
       where were
    where are
       when
Andromeda
    we know the were of you
from the light that star-started
          towards us
one million five hundred thousand
          years ago
but where among the galaxies
       are you now

where
    where am I

<229>

SKIPPING EASY

CORNFLOWERS WINTER

Where the cornflowers were
   by the thruway near the Church
Where the cornflowers
     blued the underbrush
   cornflowers bits of sky lint
Queen Anne's Lace holding its shape
in the brown-dry of winter
Those withered wisps
   they could be cornflowers
where they are
   where they were blue

SKIPPING EASY

Skipping stones
   skip   skip   skipping stones
I reverse my reel back to the easy skip
     frog skip
   onto the lily pads across the pond
stars for skipping stones in the night

<230>

ZERO

Lean one from India
    from the snows of Kashmir
Don't go up to the tower
    The sign reads VISIBILITY ZERO
Everyone is turning away
        from the ticket window
    The city will not lie at your feet
    like a snow leopard
No sea gulls will fly the rivers below
    The sea will be nowhere
You won't be supreme in the upper winds
    Read the sign   VISIBILITY ZERO
Your dark eyes of deep soundings
    gaze beyond me

But nothing is what I wish to see
I am going up to the tower.

STARS WHAT TO DO

I pick stars out of a brook
Plover at the shoreline
I beak stars from wet sand
    gather a basketful from the bay
    turn them into skipping stones
quilt them into my day jacket

<231>

ENOUGH

Isn't it enough
   you are out in this November
   you are walking down the street
     Isn't it enough
   to note the patterning
   of branches without leaves
sky pressed between skyscrapers
   to grapes of indigo
Isn't it enough
   to smell the spices down by the docks
   juice into an apple
   touch the bark of the sycamores
     peeling to lime green
You can hear the bells of noon
   through lunch-hour footsteps
You can walk out
   walk out into November

<232>

DOOR WIND

Somebody at the door
   Only the wind   the wind
      sit back down
The wind is shaping   coloring
    to someone   someone
Nonsense   no one
Could be asking me to go sailing
No one   no one
Could be a package
Somebody I used to know

No   no one

Might mean a change of fortune
Utter nonsense
I can almost hear   *Come*   come
Come to the concert across the hill
Come to the opening of violets
No one   absolutely no one
Then I'll let in the wind

<233>

COLUMBUS DAY

Pencil   flying spirit Pencil
    as the sea colds,
Will I swim into Columbus Day
fingers so numb after the tingling,
    I can hardly button my blouse.
Columbus Day
     my brother drowned in the lake
       of sudden storms
The sea is truer,
you know how deep   how fierce
Bottomless lake,
    his body never found,
any day he may be at the door
    in his blond strength:
Shelley drowned in lake waters,
someone is always drowning
    in lake waters as innocent as
      forget-me-nots
Brother   Brother
    blithe spirit Brother,
I started out flying today
     on my golden yellow
only to fall in to chill waters

<234>

MOON EMPTY

The greenhouse is going
    Greenhouse in the brownstone across
       Greenhouse lighted in the night
    Ferns golded
Young birches gold-greening
    up to the slanted roof of glass

This winter-wind day
    crates are stacked like cornstalks
The plants are leaving
    Spring of winter leaving
       Gone by dusk
The greenhouse flat with floor
    Moon-empty in the night

<235>

HOPE
OF AMETHYST
(1986)

IN THE WOMB

Singin' in the womb
     just singin' in the womb
so a news item tells us
     A nurse bending down
       hears a baby singin' in the womb
         just singin' in the womb
When a baby smiles at us
     we're told it's gas
Perhaps singing in the womb
     is gas   just gas

SUMMIT AGAIN

Summit Conference
     by the lake of Geneva
Once I walked its peace-green banks
     as a child
snow-peace of far mountains
     cow bells sounding some high valley
air to clear the heads of those in Summit
     Lake Geneva shaped like a piece of jigsaw
Walked child by the lake
   before the jigsaw summit

<238>

COMMODIOUS

Chamber music among the chamber pots
    Bit of biog turns Beethoven's bust
        Into a chamber pot
Which he kept under the piano
        Unemptied
Thereby seating his music in the bowels
    But then in the Bible
Somebody's bowels are always being moved
    A chamber maid Beethoven's need
Though a woman running in and out
    Could result in clean chamber pots
        Murky chamber music

COULD YOU TELL ME

Nobody knows the names up here
nobody knows in this flowering tree crowning
     summer resort of alpine slides
      roaring springs   false waterfalls
      cement caves   fake tidal waves
Nobody knows the names of things
     growing   grown
Those hanging baskets hidden within
     a leaf ball of yellow blooms
What do you call the flowers?
     Wish I knew.
That circle of trees way up to the sky
     birch-like bark but brown
and instead of bending over in their slimness
     they are straight as telephone poles
You don't suppose they're birches, do you?
     Don't ask — I grew up on a treeless street
The hillside thick with purple bloom
like clover except for the leaves
     Vetch   do you suppose?
I ask the thrill-ride guard
     I have no idea
Those minute red florets hiding in the barley
   by the Cliff drive —
Nobody knows by the thrill rides   water slides
     nobody knows

<240>

GOOD THURSDAY

Comics every Thursday
   every Thursday at the red and yellow comic shop
   down in the meat-packing district
Coming Thursday   the latest in Marvels
   Epics   DCs
Shop in the cozy smell of pulp paper
   printer's ink   dust mice
scarce room to stand
scant light to read the squint print

Such biographies
   Cobra   real name Klaus Voorhees
            occupation   former research assistant
            now   professional criminal
   Constrictor   place of birth Racine Wisconsin
   Controller   place of birth
            Kittery Point   Maine
   Corruptor   former factory person
            Smyrna   Delaware
   Bombshell   professional criminal
            turned juggler
            place of birth Scarsdale   New York
   Dr. Octopus   place of birth Schenectady   New York
Glossary included   *Psionic e.g.*, psionic powers
           See *Psion*
   Pym   particle   a theoretical particle
              that enables size-changing and
              mass-shunting
Every day is comic day for collectors
   of mint condition rarities
under the rusted tin ceiling
   priced as high as fifty dollars
   one sported forty-five thousand

<241>

Kids hurtle in to trade their not so new
    for the newest
climb over stacked records
bump into bulging cardboard cartons
kneel at milk crates
overflowing with *X-Men   Archies   Jaguars*
wait for the van
double parking beside meat trucks

AT ONCE

Come here   young lady
come flying your blonde hair
    singing your folk songs
No death excuses
    it's been three Easters now
Come responding to Johnny Cash
    while loving your Jackie
Come to me not as eye burning light
    not as air   not as silence
I'm as weary of silence
    as of blank blue sky
Come as the you
    I named into existence
Listen when I'm talking to you
Come to me at once
    I'm your Mother

<242>

VOTIVE OFFERINGS

Orange procession up to Roaring Springs
Kids at Action Park for speed thrills
climb reverently with orange tubes
    up the shadowed mountain
    for the rapids down
Holy procession bearing sun candles
    up into the rocky dark
Holy Holy Holy
    Lord George almighty
World Without End
    in orange Amen

SEX OBJECT

A girl wants to be
    You know
    Cherished
Like in the old movies on TV
    Like the old song albums
Not a guy ever made me feel
    More than one of them sex objects
Until just now
    At the bar where I work
      Not topless   mind
I felt
    You know
    Cherished
When a guy stood up to some punk
    Who could've knifed him
And let him have it:
    Lay off that fucking language
      Around this fucking girl

<243>

BIG BLACK

Blue peony   my wife calls me,
    I'm that black with blue overtones,
       And I play a gold sax.

My wife,
    Her hair is the red of autumn field grass;
The color in her skin comes and goes
       Like peach buds that can't quite decide to bloom.

Reincarnation is my rhythm,
    I was a black slave in another life,
       And I was murdered by my owner
    For lying with his daughter
       Under the yellow-bud tree.

I tell her this so often,
       Sing it on my sax,
    That she seems to be with my beat;
I never quite know what lies behind her opal eyes.
    Often she hides her face from me
       With her long red-grass hair.

Our two sons were formed in her white belly,
    Our sons with their milk chocolate skin.
She plays classical piano in her music-school way;
    My sax is too much for her,
       My finances   too.
    When I have it   I spend it;

Down times I work on a loading platform
    With my big black slave's body;
She addresses envelopes at home
    To be close to our boys;
       Has a piano pupil or two.

<244>

Earth this day
     Is tons heavy on me,
I was over in the Park playing my sax
     Along with drums and a flute from the band;
We hadn't quarreled
    No such thing as another chick,
Not with our love from the days of my slavery.
    While I was singing,
She sent the two little boys across the hall,
    And hanged herself;
I had to cut her down from the closet pole,
    Her petal face choked purple.
It was then I felt the weight of my blackness,
    I let out a jungle cry,
      And ran,
    Ran 'til I dropped to the curb.
The cop who picked me up
Thought I was on a trip.

I will live through whatever lives
     To be with her again;
I may even be white by that time
     In a black Empire;
Murdered all over again
    For daring to lie beneath the yellow-bud tree
      With the blue-rose daughter
        Of a black leader.

Mixing her ashes with pink petals
    I scatter them blue-grey
      On the wind.

<245>

HAPPENING

Cherry little
       cherry little footsteps
My little boy spills his cherry ice
      to the sidewalk
      from its fluted paper cup
says I'm making little cherry footsteps
little cherry footsteps all down the street
      cherry cherry
      our cherry now

ONE HAIR

Even in one   one hair
there are a thousand golden lions
      lotus wisdom of the East
If   even in one
  then   oh then
even in my piano hands
    ten thousand flaming egrets

<246>

AM A LEGEND

Monstrous tiring
     to shape myself into a legend
       less time to paint
painter among many painters now
but as a legend can I burn my name into time
     not easy becoming a legend
     when your fire is all in the canvas
No one must know I am kind by nature
     more listener than ranter
     the stuff of Gray's *Elegy*

In danger of high blood pressure
I'm starting by stomping up the Guggenheim ramp
     and rescuing my canvas
     from a wall of inferiors
Shy me   I walk around dressed like Rasputin
let it be known I get my kicks
     from women urinating on me
     bisexed of course
     into S M
murdered a man in Brazil
am an illegitimate son of an illegitimate son
my pictures are beginning to sell
     what ones I have time to paint
     while living a legend

<247>

THE GREEN

The one green tray
twenty down from the brown
    our little son in the cafeteria line
        wants the one green twenty removed
No   not possible
we move along with the brown
        his tears crystaling
woman in charge of trays
        sweating woman
        lifts the twenty in stout arms
hands him the green one

SEALED WITH MARIGOLDS

Marigolds in your gun barrels
We women seal your fire barrels   deathbarrels
    with marigolds   many-petaled marigolds
Around your necks we hang the love scent
    of jasmine
Don't crush the jasmine
    lifting rifles to your shoulders
Don't blast the flowers
    from your gun barrels
We plan to keep your guns forever sealed
    with marigolds
    your shoulders scented with jasmine

<248>

SOMETIMES I THINK THEE

Over ham-on and burgers
    We two skewer fellow poets
Mention how one doused in Rimbaud
    Tries to set himself afire
Another thinks he is T.S. Eliot
    Yet another copies Dylan Thomas
Others rhetorical   didactic
    Unstructured   too structured
Sewing circle   ho hum
    Wildly disordered in the name of dada
All the world writes lousy poetry
    Save Thee and Me
And sometimes I think Thee is a little lousy

HARVEST

Often times I slip down the hall
    to touch the golden ears of corn
        dearest daughter
you hung on the wall outside your door
    the autumn before you died
Just knowing you were down the hall from me
    with your Jackie
was harvest enough
    I run my fingers along the golden ears
    touch   touch   you
        almost

<249>

THE SEA IS NOT FAR

The sea is not far
      in this new place
the sea is not far and the hills are almost mountains
      I saw a belted kingfisher
on a New England stone fence lichen'd green
      Across from the red brick post office
a white Church from my child days
      spires the hill

In this new place the sea is not far
Names on the gravestones almost worn away
Sun and moon on a seesaw in this late afternoon
      cows across the fence
are eating out of a wagon
      not quite as black and white
      as on a hillside
        and they smell
Good old red barn by a pond algaed green
Work for the night is coming
Work for the night is long
      In this new place
      this New England
the sea is not far

<250>

HOPE OF AMETHYST

Amethyst faceted within tissue
your words faceted on the white card
Legend has it if you place an amethyst
    under your pillow
you will dream a beguiling dream

In my dream I was at the opera
    with my man of the moment
when I realized my camera was missing
and ran out of the opera house
    to amethyst rain rushing the gutter

A woman   badly pockmarked   knew nothing
    about my camera
Turning back, I couldn't find the opera house
    walked along a cliff
    no opera house in sight
Rather a fun adventure even though my clothes
were clammy wet against my skin
    delicate shoes all but dissolving
A teen gang started towards me
    Got a match?
    No, I don't
    Got scissors?
    Why scissors?
The opera house down there in amethystine light
    My man must be worried
I awaken to the amethyst under my pillow

<251>

WILLIAM RANDOPLH'S YELLOW ROSE

Tall trees toppled to William Randolph's Empire
    Hearst uprooted trees to get at people roots
        In the dung mix of blood bursts
           Tear splatters   death threats
           Bombings   sex in the closet
           Urban guerilla unemployed
Yellow journalism   blood yellow

Grand-daughter Patricia   his yellow rose
    Making news when the papers are slumping
Name that fits headline space
    Patty wanted
    Patty raped
    Patty talks
    Patty weeps
Patricia is svengali'd into headliner
    By her ghost Grandfather
Marion Davies   the wild child   no such copy
    Patricia is his news mistress
The very flower of his journalism
    Sensational

How is it with ghost Hearst
    Having his Grand-daughter a smash headliner
Perhaps turning yellow journalism to bile
    News drips out of her like a runny nose

If William Randolph had lived
    What kind of a press for his Grand-daughter
Would he have created an actress upon world stage

<252>

GROUPED AROUND A PERSIMMON
ON A CROWDED BUS

Woman with persimmon
    on a darkday bus
    orange red persimmon
        matching her scarf
Brown eyed bliss as she daintily juices
    into its fruit
sits between bites cupping her color
standees group around   questions marveling
    What is it?   A pomegranate?
    Does it have ruby seeds?
    Don't persimmons pucker the lips?

Sweet   the sweetest
    when they're red ripe
guzzled them when I was pregnant
    my baby smelled like a persimmon
        and as sweet
didn't realize I'd gone and bought
    a persimmon red scarf
No craving now
Still I expect heaven to be red orange
    while I lie back juicing down persimmons
Woman with
        paint it, someone
someone paint
        woman with persimmon

<253>

SURE

Coney   sure   it's of the mind
        the yucked-up Gowanus canal
        garbaged streets
        smelly alleys
        rotting buildings
Springtime Coney
        glitter dust allover
grass asserts itself up through
        cracks in concrete
wild flowers alongside the fun tracks
        and the sea
unswimmable in its harbor pollution
    but horizoning in seeming purity
Without a thought for Coney
    Spring hasn't happened

Coney mind sure
Coney of the thrill rides
    that terrored me
Coney of the child I was
    big brother who was
    sure legend through the revolving barrel
marveling   I took the safe route into Steeplechase

Coney on the mind of my little boy
To Coney   to Coney   my now in him
sees through a haze of cotton candy
    the bubbling of soft drinks
Merry-go-round not exciting enough
    for his nine years
The wonder wheel   will it be too tame
Nathan's   the Queen of England came to visit
I inform him between bites of hot dog

<254>

Barkers in losing competition to high tech noise
I seem to hear a street car from before
gleaming track bits through the asphalt
    where the street car curved back to Brooklyn
The piano player in the red suspenders
    and battered straw hat
    still there for me to shoot
My boy hurries me on to the video games

Salt of the sea past cooking grease
We climb rocks slippery with algae
    lean down to the barnacles
    laughing at splashes
His now   my now   in him
    Leaving him at the Cyclone
I ride the merry-go-round
    to my mind's Coney

PINEAPPLE LIGHTS

Pineapple globes spiny with light
    grow in Grand Central Station
vast ceiling blue misting star forms
    Pegasus   Andromeda   Orion   Taurus

Pineapple globes needle me   juice me
    back to meetings   partings   meetings
Do you hear me up in the zodiac
though we were lost to each other
    long before the fact of death
The pineapple globes   they're holding me
when I must get going to Track Twenty-Six

<255>

HALL OF HARPS

i
Daddy Boy, buy me a harp
   harp of purest gold.

But Cherry Baby, you said
if I bought you the amethyst earrings swinging pearls,
   you would never ask for another thing.

A harp is more than just a harp,
it's golden light to shine our downcourt place.

Why, I've barely enough room for you.
We don't live in Tara's halls .

Since you can't ever marry me, the least you can do,
is buy me a harp, a harp of purest gold.
Shine up your eyes, Daddy Boy
If you won't buy me a harp,
   at least let's look at them.

Here it is, Daddy Boy, the hall of harps,
green marble slippery as a skating rink,
cloud carpets and red velvet ropes
   like swings over to the harps.

What is your least expensive harp, Sir?

Daddy Boy, That's not how you speak of the celestial.

"This Troubadour is a good buy, a modest $900.
We can work out liberal terms,
   such as rental with an option to buy."

If the cost-of-living bonus goes through,
   I might just afford the Troubadour.
Could you recommend a good harp teacher?

<256>

You're trying to make me into a Ganna Walska,
    like that man, Mc—, Mc—

McCormack — I don't have his millions.
I'm only a mailroom manager,
but I'm willing to buy you a learner's harp.

Must I play it? Must everything be used?
Why do you suppose I ran away from my burdock town?
When you took me in, and fed me like an undercar cat,
    you knew I didn't come here
    with the least talent, only with a wanting.
Oh, this is my harp, it must have been mine.
    in another, a castled life.
See how the fluted column rises to a golden flower,
    an open cup of light,
the curve of the neck graceful beyond swans,
    pyramid old as Egypt.
It will gold me into a ray of light,
and I can go cosmos anywhere.

Could you quote me a price?

Dear foolish Daddy Boy,
How can the priceless have a price?
    It's the harp of heaven.

"Eleven thousand, three hundred and fifty;
Another five thousand for gilding and finishing."

Daddy Boy, you're losing your footing.
You'll hurt the harps if you fall against them.
We'd better get out of here before you keel over
    with a stroke.
If you don't let me have my harp,
I'll sicken, and die

<257>

I'm no Onassis, and you're no Jackie.
I took you in, and fed you,
brought you back to health.

But you can't marry me, can you?
So you have to keep me happy.
    Ask if they'll take a down payment.
I'll sell the amethyst earrings you gave me.

"Credit terms can be arranged."

Credit terms you say,
    when I couldn't buy from starvation.

You said you'd keep me better than in a pumpkin shell.
You mentioned a golden castle, which this harp is.
    See how it towers?

Couldn't buy it if I wanted to,
    wouldn't if I could.

ii
Take me to the hall of harps again, Daddy Boy.
I know you can't afford eleven thousand.
I just want to feel the ice-rink marble under my feet,
    the red velvet ropes in my hand,
and see the golden light of harps on this grey day.

All right, I'll bring you in from the grey
    to the hall of harps

Our country runs on credit, you said.
Can't we have a little credit, Daddy Boy?
I don't want to bounce about the moon,
        I just want a harp of gold,
      its neck lovelier than swans,
        a golden flower
      opening atop the column

<258>

I want the harp of heaven, Daddy Boy.
I'll sicken, and die without its light.

Here, Cherry Baby, I made some broth
    from the juice of filet mignon.
    and toasted some sesame rounds.
You'll never be up and about if you keep refusing food.
      Eat — drink,
and I'll take you to the hall of harps again.
I might even make a certain down payment
      on a certain golden harp
      with a flower-cup of light,
      and a neck lovelier than swans,
if you'll promise me faithfully
      not to ray off into the cosmos
        away from me . . .

<259>

PIANOS TO DUST

Pianos   in the music school where I work,
    I keep them dusted   floor to floor,
Come with clean cloths and scent of lemon wax,
    Dust and wax to lakes at evening.
        The wood sings.
I'd rather dust a piano
    Than play its grinning keys,
Not easy to dust the fluted music racks
    Nor the strings and pegs,
        The intricate gold insides,
    But I have it mastered,
However early I come in the morning
    To rub the sun in,
Someone is here   practicing,
    Over and over   over and over,
Rolling tone stones uphill.
Dusting   I sound the keys lighter
    Than their practice.
Dusting   I am sure of a good performance

HAVING TO DO WITH TEARS

Much water around here
    the bay   the sea
    waterfalls   and all those swimming pools
My tears salt as the sea
    but the sea doesn't need them
    I don't need them
You   my gone daughter
    lived the sea with me
As a little one you cried me in
    from way out
and now I am crying you in
    from far waves

<260>

ACTION PARK SHADE

Up in Action Park
Up the mountainside
    by man-made water slides and tidal waves
I loll in the shade of wild grape leaves
    finger the tight little   hard little   grapes
    watching the people sweating up
    to the devil's leap   tarzan rope
        roaring rapids
watching some limping back down to the valley
    or carried down on stretchers
From the shade of my wild grape leaves
    I reflect on speed as the mountain cools

TOO BAD

This doll in the closet
of what used to be the sewing room
I came upon her in a try
    at you-can-go-home-again
A china doll with holes where the blue eyes
    should be
I shook her and the eyes rattled funnily
    inside her head
My dolls' eyes were always falling
    inside their heads
impossible to rattle them back into their sockets
Guess I sort of poked the eyes out
am still something of an eye-poker-outer

<261>

AMONG SEA FEATHERS

The Fen[27] is where I go
   Fen down Boston way
any male to any male for a faceless quick one
     among the sea feathers
     quick as a gull's swoop
The fen is jaded
    oozes like a sore

Other night near the light pole
    the sea feathers parted
    to an Oriental face
his almond eyes entered into mine
    in all understanding

According to the rules of the Fen
we must play stranger
    although his touch
    was as sea feathers

Long after I searched for him
    along the pebbled path
but he was nowhere —
    The Fen no longer knows me.
      I no longer know the Fen.

---

[27] The Boston Fens have always been notorious as a place for anonymous night-time trysts.

<262>

DEATH NO DEATH

Death   give me death
        not liberty or
        not my death
Give me death as a child lives it
        my nine-year-old and his friends
Let me play their war games
arm Jedi and GI Joes with bazookas and laser guns
        grenades   light sabres
back them up with millennium falcons
        Ty fighter   X wings
        rapid fire motorcycles   laser hauls
kill   kill   kill   kill
Not a qualm nor a tear
        the dead never died
the boys pick them all up to do battle again
merry merry death   child style

LUCENT

Pearl in the oyster
        I am
am the rosy pearl
        worth diving for
Here only because an oyster
        was irritated enough
to bring me into being
here waiting in my lucent nacre[28]
        for a diver
        who may never find me

---

[28] Nacre: mother-of-pearl

<263>

A LEAF   A STONE

Flying pencil   spirit pencil
        sharp ended for words
flying toward meaning
A leaf   a stone   a door away
    Wolfe's words at the flying start
A door away and never found

Found
        in the leaf
the veinings of a leaf
Found
    in a bonfire of   leaves
        the roll and tumble down a leaf pile
Father tended grape leaves
    in our city arbor
Ailanthus   tree of heaven
leafing the window of my apartment
    in the bigger city
    of my keyboard sweat

A stone   a stone away
Found in a stone   water smooth
    shale of a long dried stream
    tranquility stone in my palm
A doorway
Found in never opening
        a leaf a stone a door
    forever found

<264>

LOST MY EARRING

Lost
   My earring
        My treasure,
   Your gift of love,
I retrace my steps,
   Zigging   zagging
Toward the three-flower fountains
        Of the Plaza[29]
Where I said goodnight to you
   In the February twilight
And went on to dinner alone
   While you caught your commuter train

The trafficked cross street
   Glisters with oil droplets,
Any one could be my petaled earring,
   So could broken glass bits
        Under the mercury vapors,
First day at the office
   As I stood in the elevator
Fluffing out my wet hair

What was it you said?
Something about me running between the raindrops,
We laughed and we were on our triangular way

   Lost earring,
      Could a loss be more fragile?
Nobody can post it on a parking meter like a glove,
      Even if I find my earring
        The petals may be crushed,
   Still I retrace,
      A slow-stepping choreography

---

[29] The fountain at the Plaza Hotel at 5th Avenue and 59th Street depicts "Abundance" in the form of Pomona, goddess of gardens and orchards. Although the base of the fountain does not depict "three flowers," it has a three-level rosette floral emblem that resembles a floral bud inside a flower, which in turn is inside another flower or calyx. This may be what Glen is calling "three flowers."

<265>

Toward the three-flower fountains
Where we are always parting,
Our moon shines by office day,
Noon our night
In a gourmet little place
Away from office eyes,
Sometimes our light burns late
After hours
What's that glittering by the shoe store?
Only a candy wrapper,
Our love is a candy wrapper
Only a candy wrapper
I backstep to this silly ditty,
The office is where you want me,
Fronting while you sit prince smiling
At your desk that shines like a lake at evening,
Your work hung heavy and I made it light,

You may even go through with the divorce
To keep me at the office,
And I would stay for the going home,
The folding into your love

Frail reeds
Leaning on each other,
I will play at seeming
As long as you play at seeming,
Yet you want to get away from what I want of you
Just as I want to get away
From what you want of me,
I want you   I want,
Candy wrapper
Candy wrapper
To a melting away bar

<266>

Could have dropped off
   At our kiss by the fountains,
      The three crystal flowers,
Stop it   stop retracing,
   Go back to your room,
You can't keep tracking back in the night
   For a maybe earring

SPEED DIO

Out from the wild grapes of his mountain
Dionysius leaps out to the Alpine slide
   of Action Park
   wrestling tidal waves
   swinging Tarzan over ponds
riding waterfalls   rushing the roaring springs
   inciting to orgies of speed
before sleeping it off
   among the wild grapes

ON HIS WAY

Man up there on the mountain
     man walking
     urging on
a tree man darkly green
   he must be on his way
   to a Summit Conference
the tree man

<267>

EYES OF THE PROPHET

Out of the fluids
behind my closed lids
    Schumann's *Prophet Bird*[30]
    fire feathers in the forest dark
    eyes of lapis lazuli
high of crest   long of feather   misting tail
    bird of my eyelid's creation
        by way of Schumann

GENEVA WITHOUT DIPLOMACY

Summit Conference[31]
    by the lake of Geneva
diplomacy a no-show unicorn

In my teens I went summer walking
    along the lake with fellow tourists
Mother   son   and daughter
    exquisite family portrait
blond as afternoon sun on mountain snows

Deep in student talk
    bending toward one another
we must have outdistanced the mother and daughter
    turned to find them gone
No way diplomatic
    in the city of the Summit

---

[30] Robert Schumann's "Vogel als Prophet" ("The Bird as Prophet"), No. 7 from his *Waldszenen (Forest Scenes)*, Op. 82, composed 1848-49, a short piano piece of incredible delicacy with a haunting bird-like melody embellished with trills. Glen doubtless learned this piece as a budding virtuoso.

[31] The first international Summit Conference in Geneva was held in 1955, with the U.S., Russia, France and England as participants.

<268>

I awakened in the Alpine morning
    to a three-way blondness
    cold as mountain snows
Mother and daughter fenced him away from me
    I walk Lake Geneva alone

T. R.

Teddy Roosevelt
        Father of all teddy bears
The Natural History Museum ennobles you
        Bronze horse   bronze rider
      at the grand entrance
small Indian and black man at your protective feet
    You charge up San Juan   San Showoff Hill

Theodore   your words sanctify the halls
      Reverence for all furred and feathered things
when your hunting hat hangs on the elkhorn
      trophy of your hunt
snowy owl collected   mounted and presented
by the T.R. who nobly refused to shoot
      a disabled bear cub tied to a tree[32]

Birds look better in the swamp than on ladies' hats
    your words blazon the walls
I hate a man   can quote you   *who skins the land*
    "Teddy's in the cane-brake"
    says a cartoon of affrighted animals
Said at Sagamore Hill   we love all things beautiful,
trees and brooks and horses and rifles and children
So Teddy shoots his animals
      and has them too[33]

---

[32] The spared bear cub became the basis for the "teddy bear."
[33] Roosevelt and his fellow hunters killed more than 11,000 animals, some of which became specimens for the Museum of Natural History in New York City.

<269>

MOONSTONE

Clever me
I proceed to outwit
the tears sharp-chinned death would pelt at me
Someone else must remove
    my young daughter's clothes
        from the closet
shoes in her footprints
mittens for hands always purpling with cold
No one can force me to go through her papers
I blind myself to her collection of *Littles*[34]
    give away her guitar
only to find at my feet a lost earring
    from years ago
The cat must have batted it about
    tiny moonstone set in silver
I am caught by a stray earring
    into a moon cascade of tears

BROKEN ANKLE

Silver pins   silver pins
    his fantasy begins
My little boy's broken ankle
    needs pins   silver pins
Time to take out the silver pins
He draws back at the sight of the pins
    poking through his skin
Asks the bone doctor
    if he can keep them to show around
    in the importance of pins
        seeming silver pins

---

[34] *The Littles*, a series of children's books by John Peterson, popular in the 1960s.

<270>

BONE FESTIVAL

Fireflies   June starting
   Here a glow   there a glow
      everywhere a glow   a glow
   on the lawn of the Natural History Museum
Night of the museum bone cold
   skulls of the hunters   gatherers
   grim men in their war canoe
while fireflies light the grass   the trees   the bushes
   in lawn festival

PURRING

Flying pencil
      flying spirit pencil
rhythming my white cat purring
purring the grey tones of sea waters
setting me down on a rock of granite
      sun warmed
surf too autumn-cold for a swim
my spirit pencil dips me into the corolla
     of tulips in psychedelic patternings
     We're above the Zuider Zee[35]
     rounding the rainbow full circle
up to the ice rings of Saturn
     Flying pencil return me
to the grey toned purring of my cat

---

[35] Zuider Zee, inlet of the North Sea above The Netherlands. The printed text reads "Zeider Zee."

<271>

HANG ON

A great wind comes up
    tortures the trees
rips roofs of houses

A great wind comes up
    scattering horror headlines
    in newspapers of the world
knocking guns from the grip of terrorists
    storming blood in tidal waves
battering the blue marble globe
    Hang on if you can
    Lash yourselves to the wind

GROWN AND GONE

Woodland of little dresses
    fluffing the racks
I dream-shop for my five-year-old
    on my way to the icecream place
That striped pinafore a love
but a bit too cutesy for my forthright child
    in her daisy yellow whippertails
The grey velvet   Yes
    but all that lace
I touch the accordion pleats
    stroke ribboned sleeves
Could hug them all
    the saucy little dresses

Grown and gone
    gone to death one April morning
I hurry down the escalator
away from ruffles and bows
    and prim white yokes
that will be hanging in the night
    of a darkened store

<272>

GLENDA AND HER
GUITAR,

EMILIE AND HER
PIANO

EMILIE GLEN

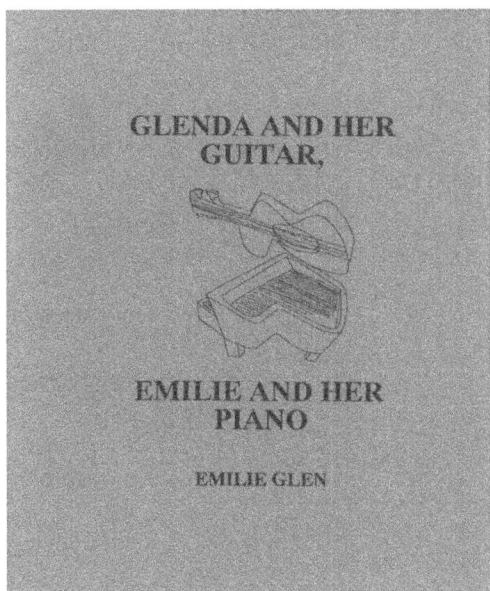

GLENDA AND HER GUITAR, EMILIE AND HER PIANO (1991)

CLEF OF LIGHT

Treble clef
  a golden chain about my neck
  emerald barrette in my hair
Treble clef on a page of music
rhythmed as waves of water
as hard to draw as to learn to tell time
I trace a treble clef in the summer stars
Shapes everywhere
  a peach the quarter moon
  boulders brioche china bell
but for me the shape of glory
  is the treble clef
intricately simple
simply intricate
  tracery of traceries
eternal elegance of the treble clef

BEYOND

Glenda and her guitar
I and my piano
Her song earth rich   sky blown
    Her guitar   my piano
past speed of light
    beyond ash
    beyond tears

<274>

SHE WALKS THESE HILLS
IN A LONG BLACK VEIL

Daughter dear
    young daughter gone from us
I'm not up to you as spirit
    want you in person
    wheat gold hair to the wind
fingers along your guitar strings
folk singing voice I could hear down the block
    and around the corner
drawing people into the coffee house
    where you sang nightly
As you were army officers say
Come back as you were
    I command it
    I demand it
Make a personal appearance tonight

HEART BEAT

Little daughter
    your heart first beat inside me
you tumbled about like zinging baseballs
    Our hearts beat together
went on with the beat of your folk songs

Sunday last in the same hospital
    where you brought
your son to birth nine years ago
    your heart stopped beating
        mine   what of mine

<275>

SHAPE OF A GRAND

World a grand
   Lid lifted
     Triangled
   Dark polished
Shaking off the globe
   In its mahogany thrust to the skies
Pedals deep into the earth of resonance
   Mighty pianoforte
Alpine keys to an Everest of tone
   Black Forest of sharps and flats
Grand great grand
   For my tone-tipped fingers
Grand in the wind of hurricane
   Pianissimo of rain drops on birch leaves
Rack for world music
   Earth the great shape of a grand piano

ASH

Used to lie sunning on the sand
  sunning   listening
to my daughter's guitar   her folk songs
Sturdy here   golden here
   voice tiding
until her ashes were scattered to the sea

This sun afternoon
I lie staring into the sand
   when a twinkle
almost too bright to look upon
tells me it's my daughter
   in one moment of ash

<276>

PIANO

Musicians breathe with their instruments
   time their heartbeats by violin   flute   cello
Not so   they say of my piano   my grand
   when the piano is my blood   my bone
   I have fingers of ivory
If you are out of tune   I am of tune
   I yearn into you
How great I am in your grandeur
   Whenever I must leave you
   most of me is missing
I am the expanding universe
    am *you* piano
the spectrum from near violet to far red

   $E = mc^2$
   $A = E$
Ashes equal energy
   speed of light

Nancy Whiskey sung blithely
by one who lost her life to alcohol
No permission to scatter her ashes
over the Greenwich Village where she belonged
   Golden hair above the golden globes
   of the cafe that knew the gold
     of her folksongs
What about the sea   the wilding surf
   that knew her guitar strings
       her sea chanties

Now the winds are warm   we will scatter
   her ashes over the sea
Spider legged word   claustrophobia
My daughter's dread of being boxed in
Can't send her down there in the dark
   with her sun yellow hair

<277>

Every atom   every cell of her being
  must be free to the wind
Up over the sea   her ashes
  Up with the gulls
  up and up and up
  above an ocean of waters
Up   up   into the forever sky

HOW COULD YOU

Little daughter of the wheat gold hair
    young lady daughter
How could you walk out on us
    in the dark of Sunday
        Easter Sunday
    leaving no forwarding address
Death I guess can be a persuasive fellow
    A daughter is supposed to cry over me
    I'm not supposed to cry over her
    until I am a salt-sea of tears
I cried over my Mother
    isn't that sea salt enough
As it is   my tears are falling on the strings
    of your silent guitar

<278>

GARNET DAYS

My music teacher
    the Master on the hill of bells
I would climb up to the Fine Arts Building
    a great rock of unpolished garnet
    until the setting sun fired the windows
cross the old wooden boards to his grand
    the Master's garnet grand

All his pupils devout
I would look up to him for everything
    the Master from Leipzig
how to dress for the concert
what foods would make me the better virtuoso
how many dates would harm my work
His wrath mighty
    if your scales were uneven
we trembled for the bluebells of his praise

    All of us devout
        until Annette
    a lesser pupil he began to aggrandize
Curl of contempt in her finger
    when he stamped his foot   small boy
From then on Annette played the role
    of *Prima Ballerina Assoluta*
he a beaming toddler
    gurgling at her every command

<279>

She rearranged his work schedule
    forbade him to give anyone but herself
        an instant over the hour
sat in on our lessons
    imposing suggestions
The Master melted down like a plastic spoon
    in hot coffee
while we melted down to nothing much
    without the Master

MULTI RAIN

Debussy's *Gardens in the Rain*
if I could compose
it would be *Fire-escape Flowers in the Rain*
complete with bees

<280>

PLEASE

Daughter   little daughter
   please   please
stay around long enough
      to see me through your   your
         I can't bear to say
            your funeral

         When it was your Father
         you planned the least detail
How can you leave me like a paper doll
         left out in the rain
don't let the metal skies fall on me
         the earth close over
         worms through eyeholes
Please   please
   you have an infinity of time
stay around long enough to see me through
the service

SURE

Knocking around out there
         unborn
my little daughter
noting the available parents
         and picking us
Grasped my finger in sure greeting
when her petaled delicacy immobilized me
         sure   friends for life
Knocking around out there again
         called deceased
grasp my finger again
         grasp my finger

<281>

DECIPHER LIGHT

Mama   you can see me
        truly you can
if you will work at it
        as you do your piano
                truly
Here's how   Mama
Learn to decipher light
        I am light
my molecules are here
        for your assembling

And Mama   listen
When you hear the winds
        dune winds
        dawn winds
        the sound of waters
you'll hear me singing my folk songs
        and talking
                talking to you
                        as always

SNOW GIRL

Wondrous snowflakes
Whitest white
        snowflakes formed on dust point   ash point
My daughter's young ashes
chill comfort when I want the flakes
        to form a snow girl
my daughter's golden hair flying
        as she runs into a cafe of songs
        down street from the Square of Washington
        opening her guitar case and
                singing   singing

<282>

GONE

Daughter gone
        I can't make it to spirit
Come to me
        not as light a stir of air
        not as a winged cloud
        a touch of snow
Come to me embodied or not at all
No   no   I don't mean blank
        Come any way you can
I'll be waiting

HALLWAY

   Not anywhere
The old music-box
   Anywhere I know of
   A big black affair
   In the dark hallway
   Of my grandmother's house
On the hill above her village
   Nowhere but in a backroom of my mind
Whenever I lifted the lid
   The whiskered gold cylinder
   In light from the thick-prismed door
Turned to music of the Rhine
   Beneath a pastel picture of the castled river
I leaned on the cool of the marble-topped table
   And watched the teeth of a super comb
   Shake out Brahms Waltzes
   Für Elise   Midsummer Night's Dream
   So the cherubim-wreathed card read
I was never sure which
   In the listening sometimes
A train whistle searched the hills
   For something lost

<283>

WALDESRAUSCHEN

Lilacs   yellow lilacs
        Fly me through yellow lilacs
            Wet with sea salt
I am fragrant
            Am sea salt
Yellow curls to my waist
        When I sat at the piano as a child
In taffeta   that murmured
        Along with Liszt's *Waldesrauschen*[36]
Playing through yellow lilacs

CONCERTO

Amphitheater under the stars
upside down dome for my grand and me
    the notes I play taking their star places
Through the stirrings of audience
    I hear the crickets
the pinging of star bells
Concerto to burst the heavens into dawn
    toward music yet unheard
Why don't I play the notes now
form them to new stars
leaving the orchestra light years behind

---

[36] Franz Liszt's "Forest Murmurs" (*Waldesrauschen*) is the first of two Concert Etudes, S. 145, composed 1862-63, an atmospheric piece that anticipates the 20th century musical impressionism of Debussy and Ravel.

<284>

IN B FLAT MINOR

His wife sets out the chairs
    for concert class tonight,
the piano lid gleaming
    like the lake below.
A little girl prodigy arranges wild flowers,
phlox and black-eyed susans
    in a snowblue vase
while the virtuoso stands sad.
"It's more than I can do
    to hold this class,"
he says from out the British reserve
that has kept his good from great.
Top ten among pianists,
    he can fill the world's halls
with his virtuosity, his musicianship,
when he could be great beyond all others
if feeling were ever to fire his tones.

"I have just lost my young nephew,
the only son I ever had.
He was mountain climbing in the Rockies.
    We flew a kite once almost past seeing,
I used to fear for his fearlessness."

"Did he have your gift of music?"

"The harmonica was his extent.
We concocted many a musical joke.
He saw so many politicians,
He wanted to be   would have been
a statesman."

<285>

He listens for answer to his unspoken why,
    in the night fields, the lullaby lake,
    the summer wind through the elms.
Chairs begin to stir with students,
"I have just lost my young nephew,
    he was a son to me.
For him I am playing
    the Chopin *B-Flat Minor Sonata*."
He sits down to the grand,
silences the cricket-singing fields _
      with his tones,
    all of him out to his fingertips,
entering into all who listen

He comes to the *Marche Funèbre*,
    chords it to all grief,
impassions it to why why why,
    cries rage,
swims the river of tears,
    climbs the mountain of his art,
and like the Brocken Specter
    of the Harz Mountains

where the atmosphere great shadows
    a mountain climber across the sky,
he climbs from virtuoso to great artist.
Can he bring this feeling
      to the concert stage?
    If so will he be a pianist
      beyond all others?

No stem can hold a flower too heavy,
    it is a onetime bloom
      caught up in the fall,
along with the other onetime shadows
purpling beyond the mountain.
His moment of art
    trembles always in the sky.

<286>

CHAUTAUQUA

Chautauqua when
   always in Chautauqua
when it rains
   poising on Chopin's *Raindrop Prelude*
reaching for Cesar Franck's
   Prelude, Aria and Finale
toward world concert stage

Chautauqua when it rains
   back in the chicken coop practice houses
   about a field of Queen Anne's lace
sweating finger-aching practice
   at a wheezing upright
the master waiting at his concert grand
     on the hill
the master   accepting only pupils
likely to follow him
   to virtuoso heights
Chautauqua when it rains
   as it rained in Majorca[37]
world stage possible only when it rains
on the practice houses of the field
the white studio on the hill

---

[37] Majorca. Island where Chopin composed his Prelude in D-Flat Major, nicknamed the "Raindrop."

<287>

HOW DARE

You there   down the hall
don't you know you've moved in with ghosts
Heedless young girl you've no right
to take advantage of my young daughter's death
my daughter and her Jackie who died
in the tilting leather chair
What right have you to turn on the lights
at an hour when my daughter and Jackie
would be sleeping
from the street I can see the wall fixture
no longer hung with guitar strap
in bright-woven yarns
to turn them off when yellow lights would tell me
I could look in on them
How dare you padlock my daughter's door
when you leave
she always left it open
Don't you feel crowded in there
Don't you feel alien
You usurper
don't bother to be sweet on the stairs

<288>

LOSING YOU

Daughter
    my darling
I've crystallized enough tears
    over your young death
    to fill your treasure box
Tonight I will sort out my tears
many of them are for times gone while you were still here

    Playing paper dolls
Jumping in your little school uniform
    all the way to the soda fountain
Creating a snow cat
Catching a sunfish   naming her Rosetta
    before giving her a proper burial
First steps   first swim strokes
    Saying *I know all about God — Episcopal*
And how does your thumb taste
    Like like watermelon
Bending over the new patent leather shoes
    Oh   oh oh
Here I am crying over what was gone
    before you were gone
You had to die for me to know
    how much I missed the child you were

CAT KNOWS

My daughter's cat knows
White princess of the black quarter moon
   she knows all is not well
without knowing the black moon of death
   she runs from our apartment
to the locked door that always opened to her
   sits waiting for my daughter
   to take her in her arms

<289>

SAYINGS

Come upon them now
    almost a year after my young daughter
        died on Easter Sunday
her child sayings
    penciled on scraps of paper
        casually put away
after all she would be a long time here
As every hair of her head is numbered
        so in death are her words

A four-year-old boast
        I know all about God — Episcopal
followed by *I have a little sky in me*
        and *I love you with all my sky*

Night's pitch black   Milk's pitch white

    Your little eyes are my puppies

Ice cream cones taste like smothered flowers

    My home is in your eyes

Your spankings feel good
like a little rosebud being rubbed on my back —

    You can't have my comfortableness anymore
    No   no more

<290>

SUN GOLDED

My place
   beneath
      a tarpaper roof in rain
My place
   is an eagle
      with white head
   sun golded
The eagle flies me up to white-headed mountains
   above the white waters of rivers
Sun wings that will never melt
    they will feather me
      to the lighted cities
    of the globe
I have earned the concert stage
    sweat dropping to piano keys
      in soundproof rooms
My place   an eagle
a snow headed eagle

<291>

RIVER DAUGHTER

Hudson a snake about me
    Glistening green snake
we swallow each other

Hudson a chimp
    Tossing blue coconuts

Hudson sings
    To the bouncing red ball
        of sunset

Hudson Mrs. Van Winkle
    In hundred year wake
        Headed horsewoman

River munching cars
        Crumbling highways
    Allowing city towers for a time
River of red dinosaurs
    Purple grapes

Hudson daughter of mountain lakes
    Rapids deepening to broad long flow
        Toward sea ultimate
Grand pianos on its currents
    Crash into Statue of Liberty
Greatest theater in its water music
    Permitting me on her concert stage
Drowning me that I may rise up out of her waters

<292>

GIFT OF SEA GULLS

Daughter   young daughter
I'm enfolded in your gift to me
        the Christmas before you died
a down-filled snowcoat embroidered with sea gulls
        you were never quite warm enough
        your fingers waxen cold

Sea gulls on the dunes
used to circle us at our sunset picnics
I stroke the seagulls embroidered
        on my snowcoat
look up to the sea gulls in the skies

ONE MORE AND ONE MORE

Just when you think
your tears have salted down all memories
        your daughter's death soft wrapped
you come upon a horse block
        by the bridle path
where you used to sit and read
        waiting to pick her up at school
Then you know there will always be
        one more and one more   one more
        but never another now

<293>

EDUCATED

Educated taste
     Liszt dubious
Want him   want Liszt
Want to play him tear flowing grandiose

Grieg   I am supposed to scorn
Scriabin   a mere rehash of Chopin

I button into Bach
respect Beethoven's Quartets
Curtsy to Mozart
     but Liszt   Liszt I must have
     cadenzas and all
forests of velour   ruby rain   lava-lit purple
     Liebestraume all the way
Let me wallow   let me soar
let me yearn   let me burn
     into Liszt

SWIFT

Sledding hill gone
    No   you are gone from the sledding hill
        my daughter of songs
you are cosmos everywhere
    reminding me at the moment
to go down into the basement
    get out the sled
and bring our little boy to the sledding hill
    No need to take turns
she'll be part of our swift down
    bearing us up lest we dash our sled
        against a stone

<294>

SLEDDING HILL

Dead
    some say
My daughter is dead
but she gave me a nudge in the snow whirl
    to our sledding hill hurry
feel the whizzing wind in the swift down
     We know every gouge and dent
        every rock on the Park hill
from the bronze Pilgrim   sword through his Bible
    to Hans Christian Andersen holding his book
where we lie on our sleds wondering up at
       upside-down trees in sycamore seedballs
          dipping blue water skies
not up to where she might be
      for she is beside us
the slow slipsiding climb
      worth the wind whizzing down
all three of us   we are snow
        swirling snow

<295>

STANDING ROOM CARNEGIE

Standing room in plush and gold Carnegie
    where we don't stand   we sit
cozy into a lushplush rug
    up two balconies
fly our magic carpet out to the sounds of symphony
    often we wrangle a cool green wall
        to lean against
eyes closed   who needs eyes for hearing
glory sounds uninterrupted
        by eye jump from soloist
           to brasses   to strings
undistracted by the conductor's arm beatings
        Standing room Carnegie
        plushlush   cool walled
eyeless   we fly sound past speed of light

WEIGHT OF ASHES

Darling daughter
    worried about your weight
insisting your poundage be fashion right
hanging your clothes on a hickory limb
    and retaining water
Now your ashes are out on the sea wind
    an ash of yours
    perhaps on my swimming arm
particles to seagulls' wings
lightsome part of cosmic dust

<296>

DREAM I

Night of no rest
   dream I dream
Length of the keyboard
    I sweat the night storming the piano keys
      no more practicing in the day
with world concert stage beyond my fingertips
    tossed in the moon of full
I eagle the grand
   sound devil strings
fly outer space on arpeggios
   play rings round Saturn
no end to the keyboard
   no beginning   no end
white keys in the blood of my fingers
   breath of hurricane

I play   play play play
   without end amen
sleeping the night red awake
    I return limp as sea lettuce
      to the turtle crawl day

<297>

MY GRAND

Grand Duchess
    Grandmother
  Grand daughter
Grand Lama
  Grand Slam
Grand should be reserved
    for my grand piano
  Grew up with my grand

My grand moved miles
  Is ailing from river damp
Sounding board cracked
   Rending of the veil
     The temple veil
Plague of moths at the felts
   In the dust of a haunted house
Its mahogany like crackleware
   Scratches   gashes
   Bleeding white
Not enough money to put it in drydock
   For a launching down the waves

My piano   my grand
Perhaps someone will buy
Pay the thousands for reconditioning
   And it will live high above the Park
Beneath a fire glinting chandelier

<298>

SWEET GIRL GRADUATE

Your certificate   darling daughter
          I never kept you from the water
your certificate   your diploma
          death certificate in cheerful yellow
          duly signed and sealed
     You have graduated   dear one
Congratulations
     you have graduated from life

PIN GRAND

Pin piano
     after jousting with grands
I find I'm only up to playing
     a pin piano
the grand kept throwing me
     for all my hours of practice
Learned how to make my own pin piano
by pressing an octave of common pins
     into soft wood
tallest the lowest   short the highest
     wound with rubber bands
I am virtuoso of the pin piano

<299>

ON THE WIND

Too young I tell my daughter
   for lines in your lake clear forehead
Whenever you feel your facial muscles tightening
   relax and smooth the least start of lines
       Never mind
   Now you are ashes on the wind

CAN NEVER

No piano
   no grand shining sunset
      my walks music remind
No room for an upright
   in a one-room apartment
      no room even for a spinet
On my way to the daily typewriter
   I tentacle my fingers
   as I pass the music school
      laddered with practice notes

Coming home to my piano-less
   I hear music minglings into twilight
      my fingers leave me
        for the keys up there

New piano in 2B
   a child at her scales
I climb up past
   The lid   the lid can never close

<300>

GRANDS

Eighty-four pianos
  eighty-four grands
Nothing grander than a grand
  eighty-four grandiose
  in honor of the Olympics
Eighty-four males in white evening suits
  What no ladies in white pants
They're all Gershwin you see
playing his *Rhapsody in Blue*
  Victor Herbert in Castle Gardens
tried to multiply his sound
  with a flock of violins
not knowing that many violins sound no louder
Eighty grands times four
  equal Gershwin guffawing

WOULDN'T IF I COULD

Mozart's piano of walnut wood
 went for a few florins
Oh to own
 No no wouldn't own if I could
Charged with his gifts his griefs
the piano would be genieoactive
 explode me to nothing

<301>

FÜR ELISE

Für Elise[38]
  violet in the grass
  Beethoven relaxing
Why do I play it cafe nightly
when Elise holds my virtuoso fingers back
  from tornado
Requested nightly by a girl alone
   when I can glitter Liszt cadenzas
   Play Schumann's *Carnival*
   the *Appassionato*
I didn't practice six hours a day
   to stay back with *Für Elise*
    the little simp

---

[38] Beethoven's tiny bagatelle, dedicated "For Elise," or possibly "For Therese," is a piece played by every beginning piano player.

<302>

EASTER ELSEWHERE

Dead on Easter Sunday
   my young daughter
   her forsythia ponytail loosed
Elsewhere   she is elsewhere
   Where is elsewhere

I skip a stone out on Easter waters

Her guitar is in the closet
   she is elsewhere
Where   where is elsewhere
   Is it an island
I'll borrow a boat
   and row to elsewhere
Is it somewhere North of cypress
   pointing the evening sky
I look up at the seething stars
   without seeing elsewhere
     where

CAN'T I

If criminals can appeal endlessly
     why can't I
My young daughter in the death house
     executed hospital style
If criminals can
     why can't I

<303>

GIFT OF WARMTH

My young daughter
    did she know
  I don't believe she
but the gifts to me before she died
   gifts of warmth
who never could get warm
     mittens   fur-lined gloves a muff
     enveloping stole in midnight blue
       down-puffed snow jacket
     the grey of her ashes

PRECIOUS

Treasures my little daughter
    can't take with her
along death's low-way
    a cloth cat
    turtle of olive wood
    knitted doll
    skeleton candle
treasures of little value
the most precious now she's gone

<304>

PEAKED HOOD

My daughter in a peaked hood
Perky peak for one so ill
    Never to be an old face in a young hood
        dead long before
In the blue mists of forgetfulness
    I think I see her riding her bike
almost call out to her
and to someone else in a peaked hood
and someone else   and someone else
city of bikers in peaked hoods
    never my daughter

CAGE, JOHN

Nightly the John Cage[39] poster
shadow-wings the cafe stage
    I am here also
playing the piano without innovation
    no papers between plucked strings
Eyes of the diners fixing on
    CONCERT BY CAGE
  as I try to outwit balking keys

---

[39] John Cage's avant-garde musical compositions included one piece of complete silence, and others in which the piano is "prepared" by adding objects to the strings or hammers to alter the sound production.

<305>

A NAME

Want   don't want
            a name
                a name of fame
not for me an anonymous house
    on an anonymous street
so I black white pages with musical notes
towards a name   name of fame
I practice the piano aching long hours
    for here a concert   there a concert
Want   don't want   a name
When I look up at the blue slate of sky
    I want my name written up there
    but when I am with the ones I love
I want to be nameless
    downed by their ills
    leaping with their joys
    living   dying
        as ages of nameless lived and died

SKY SLATE

Blank   the sky blank blue
    a slate nobody writes on
I visit my daughter on the hospital patio
listen to her guitar   her songs
    above the many windows
    blank   blank   blue
waiting for I don't know what

Three years of sky
    clouded   cloudless
when it is written
across the blue   blank blue
    my daughter of songs
    will sing no more
        not on this earth

<306>

BELL TOWER

Bell towers   many
Bell tower   one
   by the bronze still lake
of Chautauqua at evening
My hands in my lap
   still as egrets after a sweating day
   of piano practice   towards concert class
      in the white studio on the hill

Bell tower of the lake
   just here   world here
      sky deepening
bells and bats fly out
   bells and bats and bats and bells
      and my hands in my lap
      not yet ready to play in concert class
prodigies so rampant
   I might never reach world concert stage
hands in my lap
   at evening
      dark in my lap

<307>

FOOT CONTEMPLATION

Dirty little feet
   my young lady daughter's
from her not-too-clean floors
    dust mice stuck with kitty gravel
    bit of leftover glitter
She would bounce into my apartment
   plop on my sofa
Wait wait   till I cover the upholstery
  we would chat about this and that
while I contemplated her feet with some disdain
Now in the days after her death
    What ransom wouldn't I pay
to have her endanger my upholstery
    with her dirty little feet

BATTERED

My moment upon the stage
     my moment
  mine
     such as it is
couple of raised boards
  against a coffeehouse wall
my back to the audience
I ride my piano mule
   its grinning teeth in need of dentures
storm out an obstacled *Malagueña*
   Chopin's *Revolutionary Etude*
Liszt's *Hungarian Rhapsody*
avoid pieces that depend on the dead keys

Some listen
  but mostly I play
  send out my soul on a battered piano
    play   play
        into the dawn wind

<308>

BY A STAR BROOK

My young daughter
          dead since Easter
By a star brook   that's how we'll meet
Countries   they have boundaries
then there must be boundaries
         between life and after life
In studying maps of the heavens
we find a star brook where we'll meet next Easter
       running to one another
       across star stepping-stones
We'll talk   Oh how we'll talk
She will play her guitar and sing for me
       all the rollicking old songs
       and the new

OPENING

Concerto on radio waves
   In the opening of my door
Not even sure which concerto
   Homes glimmering about the lake of time
   Live in them listening
At the piano of my home on the hill
Playing the *Moonlight Sonata*
   Out to moonless poplars
Playing above New York harbor
   In the home of my first marriage
Playing in the highrise of my second marriage
   Brownstone of here
   Where I have no piano
     But I am playing
   In the opening of my door

<309>

WHY CHAUTAUQUA

Blinding white studio
        by Lake Chautauqua
My memory sweats back to chicken-coop practice houses
        circling a field of devil's paintbrush
        and Queen Anne's Lace
I practice scales towards world concert stage
        longing to swim the lake

Why am I back in my Alice-blue gown
        trembling at the master's frown
when I have the great Atlantic to swim?
Why am I ever in Chautauqua?   Why?
    Perhaps because I never made
            world concert stage

MOTHERLESS

    Daughterless Mother
Sometimes I feel
    like a motherless child
Hear you playing your ghost guitar
singing in the silence of wherever you are
    to your daughterless
        daughterless Mother
who feels like a Motherless
        Motherless child

<310>

SINGING TONIGHT

Daughter of songs
  where are you singing tonight
your tones deep as hibiscus
  high-pure as a mountain brook
Ashes scattered on the winds
will they come together somewhere
  your ashes your songs
  somewhere sound somewhere?

SHATTERED BIRD

Christmases ago
  I lost my temper
  exploded over nothing much
hurled to the sidewalk
  whatever was in my hand
  my little girl's glass bird
She picked up all that was left
  a tail of iridescent glass fibers
  rubbed it against her cheek
Through twenty-eight Christmases
  she remembered
Would take what was left of her bird
  out of her secret drawer
This Christmas I found the exact bird
  but she died before I could give it to her
  Now only I remember

<311>

STONE WINGS

Little daughter
        a scampering four
climbed up to ride the stone Pegasus[40]
        of the Plaza fountain
flew his wings of stone above your city

Pronounced dead at thirty four
Are you riding a winged white horse
across the skies and beyond

I SPEAK YOUR NAME

Too many times
        many times many
I say Glenda by mistake
when there is no Glenda
        not here   not now
        nowhere I know of
Let the wind say your name
        the wind   the waves
Glenda   Glenda
will I ever stop speaking your name to another
        often to your little son
        Speaking your name   my way
        of never saying *was*

---

[40] Frederick MacMonnies' statue of *Beauty* at the entrance to the New York
Public Library on Fifth Avenue has its female protagonist astride Pegasus, the
winged horse. There are also four Pegasus sculptures displayed outdoors at the
Brooklyn Museum. There is no Pegasus statue at the Plaza fountain at 59th
Street, however.

<312>

RED BRICK FACTORY

Long   longer   longest
longest red brick factory
ever seen in a Massachusetts mill town

Why so long?

Once when pianos were more coveted than cars
piano wires were stretched the length
      of this red brick factory[41]
      now cut up into apartments

Not a sign left then?

Why I can hear them to this day
      the wires stretching
      toward the perfection of piano
I walk the red brick length
missing the grand from my sixteenth birthday
      sold along with the rest of the furniture

Don't they have red brick factories anymore
      just to stretch piano wires?

Inside of me those wires sing the planet
and beyond

---

[41] Long factories of this sort were actually common in New England, the most common purpose being the manufacture of nautical rope in "rope walks," the long workspace required for the manufacture of single lengths of rope of the greatest length and thickness possible.

<313>

VITAL

My daughter of the wheat gold hair
strumming her guitar strings to life
        singing life
        the gold of life
How can she be nothing
but a dull yellow death certificate
closing over the gold
with vital statistics

AND ASHES

Fireworks to celebrate
        a hundred years of Brooklyn Bridge
when my daughter lived only thirty four
bridge my daughter and I crossed many a summer
        for Coney Island fun
I watch the sky glories
        with her little son
Through the star bursts   fiery caterpillars
        flower circlets   fountains of fire
we can make out the ghost trains crossing the bridge
        We soar with the firebirds
        fall with the ashes
fireworks and ashes
        my little girl's ashes

<314>

TIMING

Little daughter
     little daughter of songs
such timing in your performance
but when you went from us
     your little boy and me
your timing was off
You overhurried to become ashes
     on the sea wind
instead of waiting for the latest

Out over   the limiting sea winds
     when your ashes
when your ashes could be rocketed
     into outer space
on an almost forever trip
     at least nineteen million years
Our star wars boy ever scanning the heavens
would glimpse faint glisterings
     as of cosmic dust

<315>

MOVIE DARK

Mozart
    his impending death on the movie screen
My dead young daughter with him
    in the flow of Oceanus round the globe
I was playing Mozart while my daughter was growing
    impudent Mozart thumbing his nose
    at the portrait of his father
impudent daughter ignoring math for folksinging

I go to no medium   see no visions
    hear no voices
still in the movie dark
    ghost shadows keep rhythming before my eyes
Could my daughter be coming through
or are they shadows from the projection room
    of someone sneaking a smoke
    or my eyes adjusting to the dark
What a good rhythming of veils
when I want only her folksinging   laughing   self

Mozart   my daughter   both with a sense
    of impending doom
Mozart composing his *Requiem*
My daughter singing   *Where have all the flowers gone*
    I stay in the dark with *Amadeus*
until the funeral cart slows along the cobblestones
    to the strains of his *Requiem*
then I stumble past the seated row
    and out into the sun sharp street
only one to leave before the end

<316>

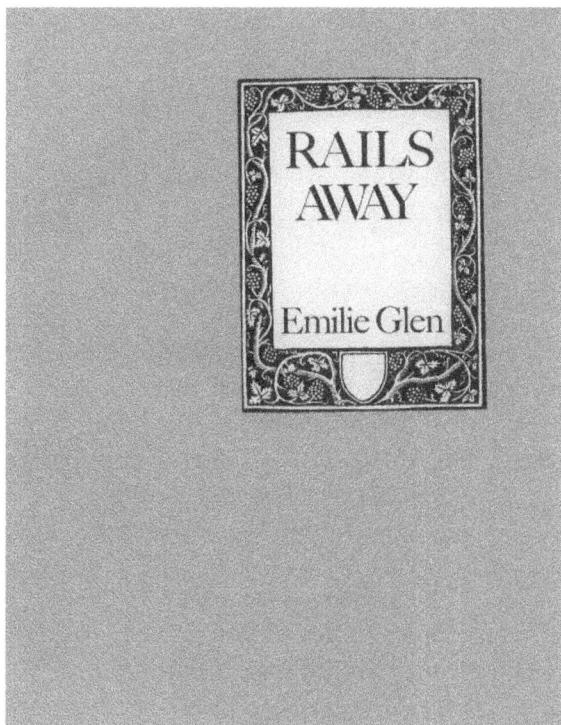

RAILS AWAY
AWAY

Emilie Glen

RAILS AWAY (1983)

RAILS AWAY

Train of child was
        The child I was
Christmas holidays in New York
        river lording
high valleys   mountains shaping the sky
Sitting all the while   swift sitting
        by motion windows
warning bells at lone crossings
steel speed past the great lifting palisades
        redbrown sunned
to the everything city   the great rainbow way
        bird-of-paradise sign-lights
        laughing away the scare dark
concerts in vast halls flashing
        prismed chandeliers
        house lights dimming
        curtain going up
        to the wide world of a play
mummies and temples   dinosaurs and jewels
walls and walls of paintings
        the rainbow city
        Christmas all around
        toys down every street
store windows in Christmas motion
restaurants in ruby candle globes
pastries of the world on silver trays

My city   mine
in the blink of a signlight
train speeding back up the Hudson
        bells at the lone crossings
rushing me farther away from window cliffs
        to the lesser town of Syracuse
for all its seven hills like Roma
        cried at the falling away of lights
Homesick going
        homesick going home

<318>

Train of the student
       past cornstalks browning
       cows on their hillsides
woods in the red   the gold   the green
wild flowers by brooks in a hurry
       train toward sky reaching towers
I'll be studying with the great virtuoso
     who accepts only pupils with
       concert potential
Wheels   faster   faster
fast as I can play cadenzas
      wheels in steel demand
     prove yourself   prove yourself
Steep palisades smalling me
     my stomach sinking   sickening
steel rails bringing students
     from all the states of the union
     to the city of greats

How can I be the one
     Back up   train   back up
     take me home
to my piano on the hill
my grand red as the palisades
     poplar leaves applauding
       my *Moonlight Sonata*
Subway poster once said
     Good is not enough
     when you dream of being great
nothing but world concert stage
     worth the ache   the sweat
Upstate my recitals were crammed
     with relatives and friends
more flowers than I could carry
     up to the terrace
     all the stars approving

<319>

Train rushing me into the sunset
      along the salt tiding river
faster   faster to the lighted city
        only the pit of my stomach
         pulling me down
my fingers ready to trace the galaxies
      tone-tell the universe

★ ★ ★

Back upstate no longer student
      train whistle loning the hills
      rail ribbons steeling
Concert class withered my hands
      all those prodigies taking over
        the keyboard
      with rhapsodies concertos etudes
My tapering fingers would split at the tips
      from long hours at the keyboard
Don't know whether the piano gave me up
      or I gave the piano up
don't know as I ride the rivered miles
      to the piano still on the hill of sunsets
Down the lording Hudson in the new year
through snow powderings towards any job
    that will let me live among the towers
      reception desk files typing pool
my virtuoso fingers trained for speed
perhaps an art gallery a music library
      can take night courses
      in Theory and Counterpoint
      write music for someone else to play
Faster wheels faster
    to a crescendo of lights
My city mine

★ ★ ★

<320>

Upstate for the holidays
snow whitening the palisades
        beyond the ribboning steel
My love beside me
        he'll be getting off at Rome
        to visit his people
I will be going to Syracuse to visit mine
and to find the lost keys   black and white
        My musical knowledge
has made me his editorial assistant
        on Quarter Notes
He the literary one   older by about ten years
        teaching me the wide world
            beyond the keyboard

Separated from his wife
separated he said
        but in the swayings of the train
        I wonder if only by physical distance
Do I care that he can never have children
Sway train sway
past snow hills where mammoths once roamed
where Rip Van Winkle slept
his hundred year sleep

               ★ ★ ★

On past the seven hills today
        past the grand piano
        past Father   Mother
        no longer the tall to my small
Steel ribbons unrolling past Syracuse
        shining on to Rochester
I'm riding with my soldier husband
        on our way to meet his family
broad shouldered exciting in his uniform
        Sergeant in the medical corps
ferns uncurling   streams in a hurry
fields of corn just starting

<321>

used to dread seeing the corn
    begin to tall off with my summer
Plenty of time for trips to Syracuse
    when he is in Korea
The old Erie Canal   buoys marking the channel
    for barges and pleasure boats
Got a mule   her name is Sal
fifteen years on the Erie Canal
Used to play around the old locks
    when we visited my aunt
saw them as ruined castles
applause of the cattails for a song I made up
        My first love printed a piano piece
            of mine
        in *Quarter Notes*   had a violinist friend
        play it at a Town Hall debut

Managing editor on *Quarter Notes*
    ever since
    he moved back to Rome
that was after his wife   in Florida
        for the divorce
    walked into the ocean one night
    deeper   deeper   until she drowned
No Venus rising up out of the sea
but a despairing   childless woman
    descending into the waters
streams still in a hurry
        wild flowers in snow bloom
    I lean into his shoulder tweed
    fragrant with peat fires

Train slowing for Rome
stopping at the station with heaves and sighs
    He kisses me goodbye
and I watch him   going through the arch
to the station like the ruins of an old castle
    The sickness   the sinking
that I had as a child when the Hudson

<322>

disappeared
his figure with dispatch case
lone through the arch
nor does he look back
Goodbye for now   for now
Swift warning bells at the crossings
as the train steels toward the night
of Syracuse
Goodbye   Goodbye

that's how she won   his wife
Sitting beside my husband   remembering
Apple knockers   we upstaters
something draws apple knockers
to apple knockers

★ ★ ★

One more time   Up the Hudson one more time
and there will be one more time
and one more time
wheels mumbling more time   more time
visiting my soldier   love
at the VA hospital in Buffalo
his lungs are wasting
Our little son reading his *Star Wars* book
Luke and Darth Vader in his pocket
Hudson in diamond ice chips
Dismal red bricks of abandoned factories
black window holes broken down sheds
We steel past the locust shells
of my mind's Rome
mind's Syracuse

Grasping at my hand   breathing in his oxygen
my husband had me promise not to let them
bury him in a military hole in the ground
there's room for me in our plot near Rochester
only Mother there so far

<323>

Past Rochester   we sing with the wheels

You'll always know your neighbor
you'll always know your pal
If you've ever navigated on the Erie Canal

  Can't we go on to Niagara Falls?
the little boy asks between brook rushes
  to the snack bar
Want to put on one of those raincoats
and go under like walking on the moon

  A deer rosy with sunset
  at the edge of a field in snow
hawks overhead splitting the sky
  with their outer wing feathers
Sing   we sing   about knowing every inch
  of the way
  from Albany to Buffalo

★ ★ ★

My love in Korea
  I come to Grand Central
  with our little son   just two
imaging his father
  even to the proud bridge
  of his nose
Under the great dome of stars
I point out to him Orion   Taurus   Lyra
  the Great Bear
  Buy a ticket for Rochester
to celebrate Thanksgiving with his
  mother and father
  to give them joy of the child
  at the brook beginning of words
Steel ribbons unroll for my little one
From the window he discovers the Hudson
  of the redbrown Palisades

<324>

the marinas   barges   tankers
mountains   like cutouts in his
     coloring book
I tell him of Rip Van Winkle
     and the hundred year sleep
Past Rome too enchanted by the boy
to wonder how it is with my first love
Syracuse just another stop on the way
      to Rochester
    Mother   Father   gone
    the grand   where?

How does his father's garden
     grow in November
Will there be flowers left for the boy
to touch   smell   even taste?
From the moving window I glimpse
     wild asters
     greenings
some leaves still redding
     golding   the woods
They'll be asking me to play their
      rattletrap piano
     when I'm sadly out of practice
I tell the little one about the snakes
     in the Montezuma marshes
show him the mucklands where his celery grows
     sing with the wheels

We've hauled some barges in our day
filled with lumber, coal and hay

    Marshes crawling with snakes
      mucklands growing celery
we sing low bridge, everybody down,
low bridge 'cause we're comin' to a town
     Rochester lighting up for us
      in the night of the slowing train

<325>

★ ★ ★

Ribbons of steel
   this summer's day
full leafing
scare trip more like Hallowe'en
even though we're on our way to the city
   between rivers
   the ocean at our doorstep
not much swimming with my soldier
in the hospital for as long as it takes
   before like little E.T.
    he can come home home

Trouble with the canister
   it's hissing away his life's oxygen
    boyman helping to adjust
The conductor wires ahead to Syracuse
   For emergency service
medics board the train with a canister
   All the while he breathes canned oxygen
   into his wasting lungs
a motion picture summer unreels
   at our window
hills seeming to abide
   tasseled corn munching cows
   fat red silos
   fireweed by streams in a hurry

We watch the indicator inching towards
   red empty
stations of the cross Rome Utica
   Amsterdam Schenectady
Albany   another team of medics
   with another tank of life
Again we are delaying the train
Hudson Rhinecliff Poughkeepsie
the indicator falling toward red

<326>

Hudson live with sails
     sun blood red over the palisades
Long wait at Harmon
my husband holds my hand
     in desperate grip
     the little boy nuzzling in
     The tunnel   the long dark tunnel
     people reaching down their luggage
for coming out into the lighted city
     We ready ours for the waiting ambulance.

★ ★ ★

Upstate for the funeral
in the fullness of August
     leaves bursting their green
Hudson alive with sails
     cabin cruisers   a yacht or two
     marinas crowded

steel rails in never meeting parallels
     to Rochester and beyond
Sitting with my boy by the motion window
I am at the piano on the hill
     playing Chopin's *March Funèbre*
salt of the Hudson in my tears
     try to crowd them back for the boy's sake
all he knows of death is to slay
     his star figures
and bring them back to life for another battle
     in ever-living outer space
Tears for my husband   share tears
     for my first love
like the two streams in France
that meet without changing their hues
     of blue and browngreen
Death train   death train
     image of a Father

<327>

who could be riding alongside him now
      free of his wasted body
Sing, Mommy Sing
      mine the voice of rubbled earth
      beneath his voice clear as the spring
at the start of the lording Hudson
        Fifteen years on the
      years on the

Steel speeding along the old Erie
my little son holding the American flag
      taken from the casket
      and folded into our keeping
I hear Lincoln's funeral train
      past dooryards where the lilacs bloom
Fields tall with corn   streams hurrying
      grasses bending the wind
no more stress   station to station
Rome   Utica   Schenectady   Amsterdam
Death train   death train
        wheels sounding   death train
      along the copper rose Hudson
        white with sails
I'll not be riding down the Hudson again
      not back   not forth
upstate earth is for graves I'll never visit
upstate earth is for rotting factories,
      gone pianos
the loved are not earthed

they live in a universe where all is energy
      that's how it is with infinity
no more back and forth   back and forth
no more trains along the Hudson   the old Erie
      The train people are reaching down
        their luggage
in the tunnel through
      to the lighted

<328>

ABOUT THIS BOOK

The body type for this book is Aldine, designed by Hermann Zapf to complement his earlier typeface Palatino. Aldine is named after Aldus Manutius, the great Renaissance humanist printer and publisher, who based his font designs on letterforms from Roman stone carvings. Titles are set in variants of Franklin Gothic, one of the great classic display faces of the early 20th Century. When this face was designed by Morris Fuller Benton in 1902, the term "Gothic" was used to describe modern-looking sans-serif typefaces, quite contrary to today's conception of "Gothic." Although the face has had many competitors, and faded from view between the two World Wars, its use resurged in the 1940s. Its distinctive letterforms and legibility kept it in type catalogs through the phototypesetting era and well into the digital era. Since it was a "hot metal" font originally, it also blends well with the urban cityscape engravings chosen for the cover. American wood engraver John DePol (1913-2004) consented to have details from four of his engravings used as covers for this series. DePol grew up in Greenwich Village and drew locales around Emilie Glen's Barrow Street residence since his childhood.

The original chapbooks from which this edition is derived took many forms, from hand-stapled mimeographed booklets prepared by the poet, through hand-bound offset-printed editions done over decades, almost all by The Poet's Press. Some of these chapbooks, such as *Late to the Kitchen,* *Up to Us Chickens,* and *Roast Swan,* had multiple editions. For each chapbook section of this book, poems have been kept in the original order as approved by the poet, except for several omissions made to avoid duplication. Many of these works had appeared in small magazines and newspapers, but Emilie Glen did not keep a bibliography. Among her papers were large quantities of tear sheets from magazines: many do not even bear the name of the journal in which the poems appeared. This leaves a large and tantalizing task for some future researcher. Volume 3 of this series will present poems published in magazines but not in this collection, with as many publishing credits as we can track down.

The first printing of this book had 454 pages and was set in oversize type. The type has been recast in a smaller size to make this edition more affordable, but the contents are the same. A few minor typographic errors and formatting issues were also addressed in this new version, released in June 2012.

<329>

www.ingramcontent.com/pod-product-compliance
Lightning Source LLC
Chambersburg PA
CBHW021352090426
42742CB00009B/827